Taunton's COMPLETE ILLUSTRATED *Guide to*

Bandsaws

D1613787

Taunton's COMPLETE ILLUSTRATED *Guide to*

Bandsaws

ROLAND JOHNSON

The Taunton Press, Inc., 63 South Main Street, P.O. Box 5506, Newtown, CT 06470-5506
e-mail: tp@taunton.com

EDITOR: Paul Anthony
COPY EDITOR: Valerie Cimino
INDEXER: Jim Curtis
COVER DESIGN: Lori Wendin
INTERIOR DESIGN: Lori Wendin
LAYOUT: Cathy Cassidy
ILLUSTRATOR: Mario Ferro
PHOTOGRAPHER: Roland Johnson, except for front cover Michael Pekovich © The Taunton Press, Inc.; p. 8 (left) © Jim Harvey;
p. 10 (left) Courtesy of *Fine Woodworking* magazine © The Taunton Press, Inc.; (right) Courtesy of Powermatic/WMH Tool
Group; p. 12 © Dan Iburg; p. 18 (top right) © Dick Streff; p. 22 (left) © Paul Anthony

Fine Woodworking® is a trademark of The Taunton Press, Inc., registered in the U.S. Patent and Trademark Office.

LIBRARY OF CONGRESS CATALOGING-IN-PUBLICATION DATA

Johnson, Roland.
  Taunton's complete illustrated guide to bandsaws / author, Roland Johnson.
    p. cm.
  ISBN 978-1-60085-096-7
  1. Band saws. 2. Woodwork. 3. Sawing. I. Title. II. Title: Complete illustrated guide to bandsaws.
  TT186.J64 2010
  684'.083--dc22
                        2010028597

Printed in the United States of America
10 9 8 7 6 5 4 3 2 1

The following manufacturers/names appearing in *Taunton's Complete Illustrated Guide to Bandsaws* are trademarks: 3M™Fast Track, Acu-Arc™,
AccuRight™, Bostik TopCoat®, Carter Magfence™, Carter Stabilizer®, Craigslist℠, eBay℠, Felder®, General®, Laguna® Tools, Olson®Cool
Blocks®, Powermatic®, Quick Release®, Scotch-Brite™, Spaceage Ceramic Guideblocks®, SuperCut™.

Working wood is inherently dangerous. Using hand or power tools improperly or ignoring safety practices can lead to permanent injury or even death. Don't try to perform operations you learn about here (or elsewhere) unless you're certain they are safe for you. If something about an operation doesn't feel right, don't do it. Look for another way. We want you to enjoy the craft, so please keep safety foremost in your mind whenever you're in the shop.

For JoAnn

Acknowledgments

THIS BOOK WAS SCHEDULED to take one year to complete, but in fact took two, so I have to thank a few folks for their persistence and patience. I want to start by thanking my long-suffering wife, JoAnn, for putting up with the highs and lows and long hours that accompany such an endeavor. Thank you, dear.

I also owe a heartfelt debt of gratitude to Helen Albert for giving me the chance to write this book and for being so patient with my tardiness. A huge thanks goes to my editor and pal Paul Anthony for keeping the reins tight and the whip handy, and for making sense of my miscellaneous ramblings. Thanks also to Jessica DiDonato for keeping track of my progress and for tending to the home fires at Taunton.

A special thanks to Anatole Burkin for being my friend and advocate. And finally, I would like to thank all of my friends and relatives who have put up with my absence. (Or maybe they should thank me.)

"Writing a book is an adventure. To begin with, it is a toy and an amusement; then it becomes a mistress, and then it becomes a master, and then a tyrant. The last phase is that just as you are about to be reconciled to your servitude, you kill the monster, and fling him out to the public."
—*Winston Churchill, speaking at Britain's 1949 National Book Exhibition about his World War II memoirs*

"The tyrant has been vanquished."
—*Rollie Johnson*

I would also like to thank the following for their help, materials, information, and advice:

Jay Andrews/Laguna Tools
Tom Bloxsom/Olson Saw
Art Gschwind/Suffolk Machinery
Steve Krohmer/Rockler
Mike Lord, Bill Stoiko, and
    Bonnie Stoklosa/HTC Products
Steve Mangano/Rikon Power Tools
David Morris/SuperCut Bandsaw Co.
Lisa O'Dell/Wearwell Mats
Nick Osa/Spaceage Ceramic Guides
Robin Palmer/Fenner Drives
Lee Perez/Carter Products
Ed Scent/Highland Hardware
Barry Schwaiger/WHM/Jet/Powermatic
Rich Whitsitt/Rockford Spring Co.

Contents

Introduction • 3

SECTION 1 — The Versatile Bandsaw • 4

5 Cutting Abilities

7 Types of Saws

11 Anatomy

20 Accessories

24 Buying New

27 Buying Used

SECTION 2 — Tune-Up and Alignment • 31

50 Tire Maintenance

52 Handling Blades

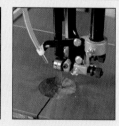
53 Table Maintenance

SECTION 3 — Bandsaw Blades • 54

54 Blade Terminology

66 Cleaning Blades

66 Storing Blades

► SECTION 4   Blade Guides • 68

79 Squaring Guides   81 Replacing Guides

► SECTION 5   Safety • 82

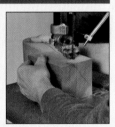

82 Know Thy Saw   84 The Bandsaw Workstation   85 Safety Gear   87 Safety Accessories   91 A Safe Stance   93 Safe Stock Feeding

► SECTION 6   Sawing Straight • 95

112 Pushers   115 Basic Cuts   117 Dealing with Blade Drift   119 Using Fences   123 Tapering   127 Two Essential Jigs

SECTION 7 — Sawing Basic Curves · 129

150 Circles and Arcs

157 Complex Curves

SECTION 8 — Advanced Cutting Techniques · 162

172 Compound Sawing

174 Curved Moldings

177 Making Tenons

184 Special Techniques

191 Slabbing Logs

Glossary · 196

Metric Conversion Chart · 198

Resources · 199

Index · 200

Introduction

BANDSAWS ARE the Jekyll-and-Hyde tools of the woodshop. They appear benign and easy to operate but can be diabolical when it comes to producing repeatable results. Many woodworkers harbor deep distrust and dark suspicions about the family lineage of their saw and suspect it of having a willful soul that disrespects any project brought to it.

But in reality, the bandsaw is the most valuable power tool in the furniture shop. It can rip, crosscut, and saw curves through thick and thin material with less waste and power than any other saw in the shop. When the right blade is installed, the saw setup fine-tuned, and the proper technique used, the stars align. Truth is, a bandsaw can perform so admirably that a woodworker may wonder why he or she would need another power saw in the shop.

This book will provide all the information you need to align those stars and make your bandsaw a joy to operate, with absolutely predictable results every time you flip the switch and run wood past the blade.

The Versatile Bandsaw

THE BANDSAW has been a mainstay woodcutting tool of lumber sawyers, furniture makers, and wooden boat builders for well over a century. A bandsaw's versatility stems from its narrow, continuous loop of a blade, which allows the saw to make both straight and curved cuts. The thin blade cuts a narrow kerf, requiring less horsepower and conserving wood. Outfitted with the proper blade, a bandsaw can do everything from cutting tight curves to ripping thick planks and resawing wide boards.

Bandsaws are inherently safer than tablesaws because the danger of *kickback* is eliminated. Kickback is a tablesaw's tendency to errantly grab a piece of wood and hurl it toward the operator. A bandsaw's downward cutting action prevents this. That said, the machine still deserves respectful caution. Keep in mind that the bandsaw is a butcher's tool of choice for cutting meat and bone.

Small shops benefit from the bandsaw's compact footprint. My biggest saw, with its 3-hp motor, 18-in. throat, and 12-in. resaw capacity, takes up only 6 sq. ft. of floor

Ripping lumber on a bandsaw can be done more safely and with less horsepower than with a tablesaw, and it's just as fast.

With its small footprint, a bandsaw occupies little space but performs big cutting duties.

A bandsaw can easily rip thick timbers, even on a 120-volt circuit.

able tool. It can do everything from cutting complex shapes and joints to slicing boards across their width to create veneers, panels, and slabs. Turners also find it a great tool for roughing out bowl blanks.

Sawing Shapes

The ability to accurately saw long, gentle curves is one of the bandsaw's greatest virtues. Used with the proper technique, it can safely cut the compound curves of a cabriole leg with little effort. Other furniture parts with multiple curves and arcs can also be quickly and accurately produced or roughed to shape in preparation for final cutting with a router or shaper. Outfitted with a narrow blade, a bandsaw can perform precise, square-edged scroll sawing in stock much thicker than a scroll saw can accommodate.

space. And it has proved adequate for any job I have encountered making furniture, crafting architectural millwork, or doing general woodworking. Outfitting a saw with a mobile base also adds great convenience. I can literally park my several bandsaws against a shop wall until needed.

Another big benefit of a bandsaw is its minimal power demands. A typical 14-in. bandsaw operates efficiently on 120-volt power even while resawing wide hardwood. A 20-amp shop circuit is best for this, but most typical small-shop cutting operations won't even tax a 15-amp circuit. Because of this, a bandsaw can be the perfect all-purpose saw in a garage or basement shop that's not wired for 240-volt power.

Cutting Abilities

It's a bandsaw's ability to perform a wide variety of cuts that makes it such a valu-

Sawing complex shapes and compound curves in thick wood is one of the bandsaw's unique abilities.

Equipped with a narrow blade, a bandsaw can cut accurate circles and tight scroll patterns with precisely square edges.

A BRIEF HISTORY OF THE BANDSAW

The earliest recorded patent for a bandsaw was granted to Englishman William Newberry in 1809. Unfortunately, blade technology was still in its infancy, and the lack of an effective method to join the ends of the blade led to frequent failures, relegating the invention to curious-contraption status. Nearly 40 years passed before Frenchwoman Anne Paulin Crepin devised a technique for welding a bandsaw blade so that it could withstand the rigors of sawing and bending around bandsaw wheels. She applied for a patent in 1846, and soon afterward, manufacturer A. Perin & Company of Paris, France, purchased the rights to her innovation. Combining Crepin's welding method with new steel alloys and advanced tempering techniques, Perin created the first "modern" bandsaw blade. In a short time, the bandsaw became a centerpiece tool in many well-equipped woodworking shops, and by the 1860s the first American-made bandsaws entered the arena.

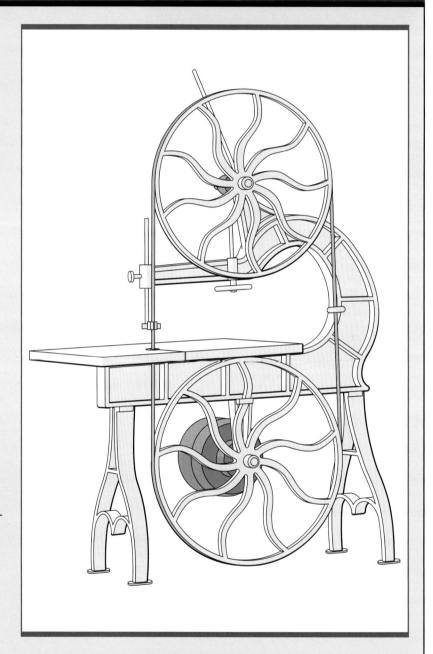

Joinery

Most joinery that can be accomplished with a handsaw can be cut on a bandsaw faster and with less physical effort. Half laps, bridle joints, and tenon cheeks are as quickly, precisely, and safely sawn on a bandsaw as on a tablesaw. When necessary, the tilting table allows bevel cutting and dovetail joinery.

Resawing

Resawing is the process of ripping wide lumber through its width. The bandsaw is the only woodworking machine that can resaw wide stock, allowing you to make sheets of veneer from valuable wood or cut matched panels for doors or drawer fronts.

Sawing Slabs & Bowl Blanks

Most woodworkers have a fascination with sawing logs into planks. There are few processes in woodworking more delightful than opening a log to reveal the hidden beauty under the bark. With the help of a simple shopmade jig, small logs can be quickly and efficiently sawn into planks, making the saw a great resource when your neighbor's pear tree blows down in a storm. A bandsaw can also quickly turn big chunks of green wood into bowl blanks for the lathe. Even a relatively low-horsepower bandsaw can beaver its way through thick wood to produce the rough shape of the bowl.

Types of Saws

Bandsaws can be roughly categorized into three classes: benchtop models, 14-in. stand-mounted saws, and large floor-model saws.

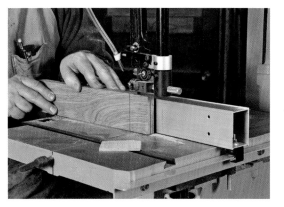

Tenon cheeks are cut quickly, accurately, and easily on the bandsaw, as are half laps and bridle joints.

The bandsaw excels at resawing—the process of slicing a board widthwise into thinner pieces.

Equipped with a log sled, a bandsaw can serve as a mini sawmill, converting small logs into useable slabs of lumber for small projects.

A bandsaw can quickly and efficiently reduce chunks of freshly cut green wood into bowl-turning blanks.

THREE-WHEELED SAWS

Three-wheeled band-saws are a rarity and a bit of an anomaly. These saws offer large throat capacity in a relatively small package but typically lack much height (resaw) capacity. Compared to two-wheel saws, three-wheelers are much more difficult to track accurately. They

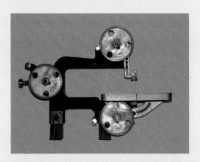

This vintage Craftsman three-wheeled bandsaw (with sheet metal covers removed) has a deep throat, but the small wheels are tough on blades, which can also be difficult to align.

can also be harder on a blade because it is bending three times for each revolution instead of twice. This small-radius bending can invite blade breakage, although using blades thinner than 0.02 in. can help minimize the risk.

You might have a hard time finding a three-wheeled bandsaw these days. No U.S. manufacturer offers them and, although Swiss manufacturer Inca used to sell a high-quality aluminum-frame bandsaw, its production was discontinued some years ago. There are still old models around, though. For more information about Inca bandsaws, see Resources on p. 198

These "types" correspond primarily to a saw's size, which correlates to the diameter of its wheels. In this book I'll focus on bandsaws about 24 in. and smaller—the typical equipment suitable for most amateur and small professional shops. Regardless of size, the setups and operations are essentially the same for any woodworking bandsaw.

Benchtop Saws

The kids of the bandsaw family, benchtop models typically sport wheels less than 12 in. in diameter. The body of a benchtop saw is constructed as a single unit with the motor integrated into the framework, making it reasonably lightweight and portable. Although limited by a narrow blade-

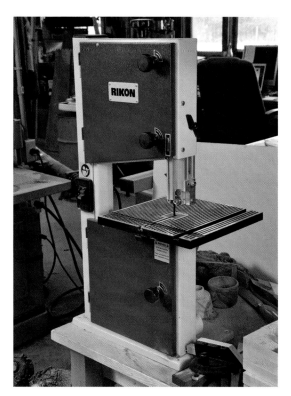

This Rikon benchtop bandsaw has all the features of a big bandsaw but in a very compact package.

width capacity, small resaw height, and low horsepower, these mites are fine for small projects, especially when sawing thin wood is the norm.

A benchtop saw's small size and low power is less intimidating for beginners and children. It can be an inviting "first saw" for those just dipping their toes into the waters of woodworking. It can also provide great service as a second shop saw. Outfitted with a ¼-in. blade, a benchtop saw is good for those odd jobs that always seem to pop up right after you've set up your larger saw with a wide blade for another project.

Some welded-steel benchtop bandsaws offer big-saw features like roller-blade guides and substantial table supports. Essentially scaled down from their bigger siblings, these youngsters are solid little units that can perform accurate cutting on a small scale. Many budget-price benchtop saws are available through online sources and at big-box stores, but keep in mind that you definitely get what you pay for.

14-in. Stand-Mounted Saws

The cast-iron-framed 14-in. bandsaw is probably the most popular model ever produced. The saw is a competent machine for ripping and resawing, although the basic machine is limited to a resaw capacity just shy of 6 in. Most manufacturers offer an accessory "riser block" to increase resaw capacity to about 12 in. The riser is simply a cast-iron spacer that fits between the two frame halves, raising the upper half of the saw. It certainly works, although an upgrade from the standard 1-hp motor is needed to really exploit the increased resaw capacity.

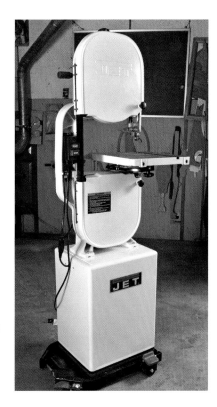

The standard-height 14-in. cast-iron-framed bandsaw is incredibly popular because it can perform nearly any bandsawing task a typical small shop demands.

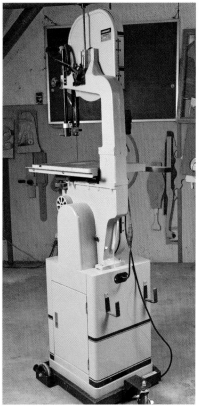

Adding a 6-in. riser block between the two frame halves increases resaw capacity to about 12 in. and generally improves the versatility of a 14-in. bandsaw.

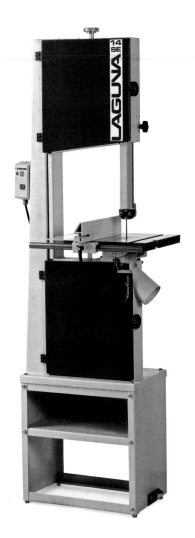

Welded steel-frame 14-in. saws (left) that offer increased integral resaw capacity are becoming more popular and more available.

With its 18-in. resaw capacity, 18-in. throat, 5-hp motor, big table, and heavy-duty frame, this Powermatic (right) is a serious bandsaw.

The two-piece cast-iron frame offers good rigidity and substantial support for the guidepost to minimize flexing. These saws are available with open or closed stands, a variety of blade guide systems, and motors ranging from ¾ hp to 1¾ hp. Saw manufacturers offer lots of accessories, as do makers of aftermarket gizmos, providing a saw owner with many opportunities to customize the "little engine that could."

Recently, several welded-steel 14-in. bandsaws have become available that offer resaw capacity ranging from 10⅛ in. to 13⅛ in. Standard features include motors up to 2 hp, as well as roller or ceramic guides.

16-in. & Larger Saws

Bandsaws with 16-in.-dia. and larger wheels offer increased width- and height-cutting capacity. They have strong frames capable of handling the high-tension demands of wide blades and strong motors for sawing big workpieces. The wheels are wide enough to accept large blades and heavy enough to ensure good momentum for moving through stock at a consistent speed. In addition, the weight of these big saws helps dampen vibration during use.

Everything is larger on these saws. Their tables and supports are bigger and beefier, providing a large working surface that can withstand heavy-duty use. Blade guides are also typically larger, offering more surface area to better support wide blades.

Although available with as little as 1¾ hp, most of these saws come equipped with 2-hp or larger motors. Some have 5-hp American-made motors with continuous-duty ratings sufficient for extended sessions ripping heavy stock or resawing.

Anatomy

All bandsaws are essentially the same, regardless of size. They are relatively simple machines with easily accessed parts that serve obvious functions. Take some time to familiarize yourself with the location and names of the various parts.

The Frame

The frame is the most important part of a bandsaw. It supports the wheels, guides, table, and sometimes the motor. A strong, rigid frame is essential to adequately support the tension of the blade and provide a sturdy mount for the blade guides. The frame material also has to remain stable through-out temperature and humidity changes to ensure accurate alignment of the wheels and guides. There are three basic types of frame material: die-cast, cast iron, and welded steel. Each type has its own particular benefits and drawbacks.

Die-cast frames are typically made of aluminum and can be produced relatively cheaply in large volumes. Die-casting is a popular manufacturing process for mass-producing machines like the benchtop band-saws sold through big-box stores. Several decades ago, most manufacturers offered at least one die-cast small bandsaw, but few

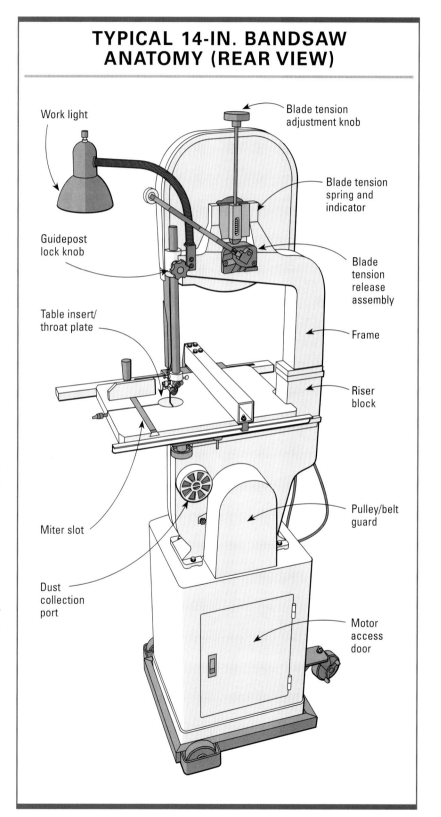

TYPICAL 14-IN. BANDSAW ANATOMY (REAR VIEW)

Work light

Blade tension adjustment knob

Blade tension spring and indicator

Guidepost lock knob

Blade tension release assembly

Table insert/ throat plate

Frame

Riser block

Miter slot

Pulley/belt guard

Dust collection port

Motor access door

Complex, lightweight castings are common in mass-produced benchtop bandsaws. These die-cast frames are typically aluminum.

TYPICAL WELDED-STEEL BANDSAW (FRONT VIEW)

Upper wheel

Guidepost lock knob

Guidepost elevation wheel

Guidepost/blade guard assembly

Guide assembly

Upper wheel house door

Trunions

Table

Power switch

STOP

Frame

Lower wheel

Motor drive pulley and belt

Mobile base

Lower wheel house door

remain in production today. Although die-cast saws were often considered to be inferior, these lightweights can perform admirably with a sharp blade, properly adjusted guides, and good work habits. Just don't expect to use blades wider than ½ in., because the frame can't take the tension.

Cast iron is a very good material for a bandsaw frame because of its great strength, rigidity, and dimensional stability. Its weight provides physical stability, its mass helps dampen machine vibration, and the metal machines easily and accurately. Two-piece cast-iron frames are typical of modern generic 14-in. bandsaws.

With its cast-iron frame and wheel houses, this old Walker-Turner bandsaw is heavy and strong.

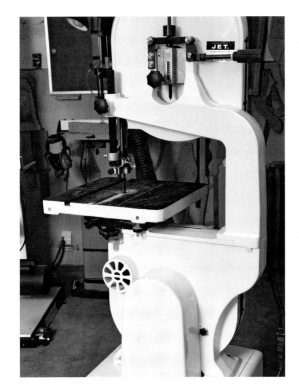

TYPICAL WELDED-STEEL BANDSAW (REAR VIEW)

Blade tension release handle

Blade tracking adjustment knob

Blade tension gauge

Miter slot

Blade tension adjustment wheel

Table insert/ throat opening

Dust port

Lower wheel hub

Motor

Stamped-steel wheel houses on this modern saw attach to a very rigid two-piece cast-iron frame, the halves of which bolt together near the table.

With the wheels and doors removed, the amount of welded steel in this frame is obvious.

Massive cast-iron wheels provide flywheel inertia to help keep a blade moving at a consistent speed through stock of inconsistent density.

Welded-steel frames are composed of sheet steel that is folded and welded to produce a rigid frame. Once exclusive to large industrial bandsaws, welded-steel frames are becoming the norm for many midsize saws and benchtop models. Welded steel is ecologically friendlier than cast iron and eliminates the need to "season" castings to ensure dimensional stability. Although rigidity (especially of the upper guidepost mount) has been a problem on some models, these saws generally represent good value, often costing much less than comparably sized cast-iron machines. Welded steel is lighter than cast iron, which offers a tradeoff of lower freight rates for less vibration-dampening weight.

Wheel Houses

Enclosures for the wheels are referred to as wheel houses. On welded-steel or cast-aluminum bandsaws, they are integrated into the frame. On cast-iron-framed bandsaws, wheel houses are attached as separate parts made of sheet metal, cast iron, or cast aluminum. Wheel house doors on the front of the saw cover the top and bottom wheels for safety.

Wheels & Tires

A bandsaw's wheels and tires provide power, support, and guidance for the blade. The upper wheel can be raised and lowered to tension the blade and tilted to track it. The lower wheel, which drives the blade, is either mounted directly to the motor arbor or connected via pulleys and a belt. The wheels, which are typically cast from iron or aluminum, are machined to accept a pliable tire around their perimeter. Cast-iron wheels,

Lightweight cast-aluminum wheels lack the flywheel inertia of heavier wheels but reach maximum speed more quickly, a benefit with small saws.

With the table removed on this saw, both the upper and lower roller-guide assemblies are clearly visible.

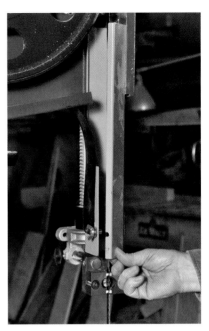

The blade guard on this bandsaw has a hinged door that allows access to the blade.

which are much heavier than aluminum wheels, create a flywheel effect to help maintain consistent blade speeds when cutting through material of varying density.

On smaller saws, the wheels usually include a machined channel to accept the tire. It is crown-shaped to aid in tracking the blade. On larger saws, the crown is shaped into the tire itself, which is typically bonded to a flat-edged wheel. Although tires are traditionally made from rubber, they are also available in urethane and neoprene.

Guides & Guards

Blade guide assemblies above and below the table confine the blade to maintain an accurate cutting path. Each assembly consists of a side guide on either side of the blade and a thrust guide directly behind the blade. The side guide prevents lateral blade twist, while the thrust guide supports the back edge of the blade to resist feed force. Thrust guides are essential for maintaining the strength of the blade. They keep it in a straight line

to prevent deflection, which causes inaccurate cuts. The upper guide is mounted to a height-adjustable guidepost that allows positioning the guides ¼ in. above the workpiece for maximum blade control and safety.

A guard covers the section of the blade between the guides and the upper wheel house. Some guards must be removed when changing blades, while others have hinged panels that swing open to allow access to the blade.

Table

The bandsaw table supports the work being sawn. It has a removable throat plate and a slit that runs from center to edge to allow blade changes. To keep the table sections aligned at the slit, a small, tapered pin is typically inserted into a hole bored in the edge of the table. Bandsaw tables are usu-

On a typical band-saw table, a tapered pin inserts in the table edge to align the sections adjacent to the table slit.

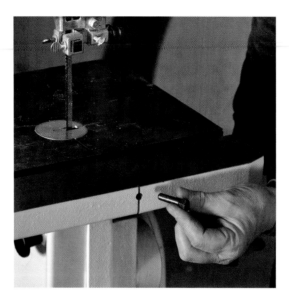

The trunnion assembly allows for tilting the table. Lock knobs secure the table at any angle up to 45° to the right and about 10° to the left.

A miter gauge is a great asset for crosscutting boards, and the movable fence accurately guides rip cuts.

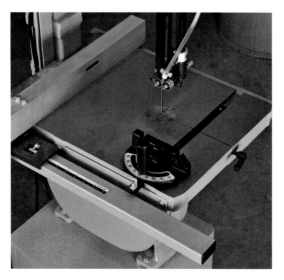

ally made of cast iron, although at least one manufacturer is now using granite. Benchtop saws normally have cast-aluminum tables.

The semicircular mechanism that supports the table is called the trunnion. The trunnion assembly rides on the trunnion support and is typically secured by a pair of bolts and knobs, although on some bandsaws a single large bolt does the job. The trunnions typically allow the table to tilt just past 45° to the right and about 10° to the left for sawing bevels. Hefty cast-iron trunnions are best. Die-cast units are not as reliable and sheet-steel trunnions are even less so.

Most tables also include a slot that runs front to back to accommodate a miter gauge, crosscut sled, or other jig. A standard miter slot is ¾ in. wide by ⅜ in. deep. Some are milled in the shape of an inverted T, like the table slots commonly found on tablesaws. This T-track accommodates a washer on the end of some miter gauge bars. The washer allows cantilevering the miter gauge off the table for crosscutting wide stock.

Rip Fence & Miter Gauge

The rip fence extends from front to back on the table. Most rip fences slide side-to-side on a rail that's attached to the front of the table. A good rip fence will allow you to angle the fence diagonally across the table-top to accommodate a sawing phenomenon known as blade drift. (See "Dealing with Drift" on p. 99.) The miter gauge has a protractor-style head that can be angled to make crosscuts or miters. The head mounts to a steel bar that is guided by the miter gauge slot in the table.

Wheel Adjusters

The upper wheel is mounted on an axle on the tracking and tensioning mechanism. The axle tilts horizontally to allow tracking a blade. The axle also travels vertically and is equipped with a tensioning screw and spring to provide blade tension. The spring also acts as a shock absorber for the blade, providing some resilience when the blade encounters a knot or other sudden change in wood density. Some bandsaws include an axial adjustment for the lower wheel. This allows for tilting it both horizontally and vertically to achieve proper alignment with the upper wheel.

Drive Mechanism

Most bandsaws are belt driven, with the motor driving the lower wheel via pulleys and a belt. On welded-steel saws, the motor is often bolted directly to the lower wheel housing. On most cast-iron saws, the motor is located above or inside the saw stand. Motor speeds typically range from 1450 rpm to 1720 rpm, depending on the vintage. Manufacturers reduce the rpm to achieve the proper blade speed by using differential pulleys, with a large pulley on the wheel and a small one on the motor. The big advantage of a separate motor is its ease of replacement if necessary. Replacement motors are usually easy to find and reasonably priced.

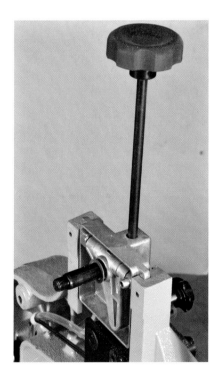

Removing the upper wheel on this Powermatic saw exposes its pivoting wheel axle assembly, which allows tilting and raising the wheel for blade tracking and tensioning.

The tensioning screw and spring on this Jet saw are clearly visible inside the upper wheel house and are an integral part of the upper-wheel axle assembly.

The four bolts on this lower wheel hub, located directly below the motor, allow horizontal and vertical adjustment of the wheel's axle on this large welded-steel bandsaw.

Power for the wheels is transferred from the motor by pulleys and a belt—in this case, a multi-V belt.

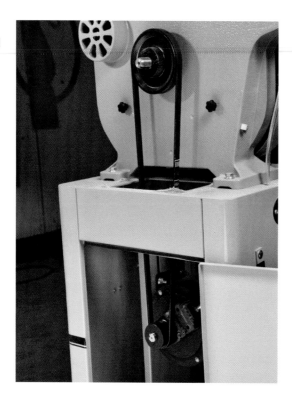

Double pulleys allow two-speed adjustment. The higher speed is for woodcutting, while the lower speed allows sawing soft metals.

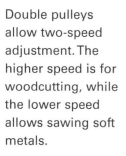

On direct-drive bandsaws, the drive wheel mounts on the motor's armature shaft, typically using a low-rpm three-phase motor.

Some belt-driven saws sport a double pulley on the motor and on the lower wheel, allowing two-speed adjustment. At its lower speed, a saw like this will do a great job of cutting soft metals like brass or aluminum, although it's still too fast to saw ferrous metals.

Some bandsaws are direct drive. On these, the lower bandsaw wheel mounts directly onto the motor shaft. The motors are typically low-speed, three-phase units that don't require use of differential pulleys to achieve the proper blade speed. Three-phase motors are more efficient than single-phase motors, reaching maximum power at very low rpm. However, they require a special power source and wiring. Also, direct-drive motors are

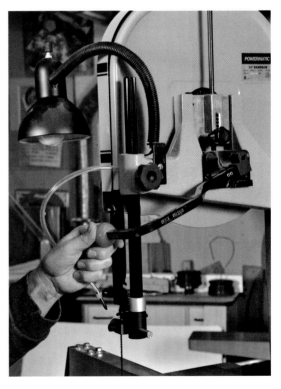

typically model specific and can be very expensive to rebuild or replace.

Dust Collection Port

Bandsaws create clouds of fine sawdust that will find their way into every nook and cranny of your saw, your shop, and your lungs. Dust collection is important not only for your shop cleanliness and your health, but also to prevent sawdust from accumulating on the tires and guides. Dust collection ports should be located as close to the source of the dust as possible, which is directly below the lower blade guides. Better saws include a ramped chamber in the lower housing that directs the dust toward the dust port. Some ramps even have a blade-surround to concentrate the dust near the collection point and prevent it from dropping into the lower wheel housing. A 4-in. dust port is best for evacuating the fine, lightweight dust a bandsaw produces. It also allows the easiest hookup to a dust collector. A 2¼-in.-dia. port isn't as effective, but it accepts standard shop vacuum hoses.

Quick-Release Tension Lever

Many modern bandsaws come equipped with a quick-release tension lever. This feature spares you lots of wrist action on a tensioning knob when changing blades or when relieving the tension on a saw that won't be used for a while.

Good dust collection includes a large dust port, a ramped chamber to concentrate the sawdust near the port, and a brush to keep the wheel clean.

A 4-in.-dia. dust port located right below the lower guides allows the large-volume airflow needed to evacuate the fine dust that a bandsaw creates.

This Powermatic saw includes a quick-release tension lever for faster blade changes or for de-tensioning a saw that will sit idle for a while.

[TIP] **Tires on seldom-used saws can become distorted from constant blade tension. If you operate your saw less than once a week, it's wise to release the blade tension between uses.**

Foot Brake

The significant mass of large bandsaw wheels creates considerable inertia. When the power is shut off, the combined momentum of the two wheels can keep them spinning for quite some time, especially when outfitted with a narrow blade. A foot brake is a great safety device as well as a time-saver. Waiting for a brakeless saw to spin down can create frustrating delays when setting guides or when frequent stopping is needed to reorient a workpiece or jig. Some foot brakes include an integral micro-switch that cuts the saw's power when the brake is applied, providing a good emergency stop.

Accessories

Bandsaws invite accessorizing. The basic machine can be enhanced by enlarging the table area, outfitting the fence for versatility, increasing cutting-height capacity (on some saws), and adding machine mobility. Some saws can also benefit from a blade guide system upgrade. And almost any bandsaw workspace can use a good floor mat.

Tables

Bandsaw tables are relatively small, which can be inconvenient when working with long boards or large panels. A big auxiliary table can make bandsawing easier and safer because it offers better support for big workpieces. Commercially available aftermarket tables often include a fence as well as a T-track to accommodate a miter gauge, a feather board, or jigs for positioning work and sawing circles.

Removing the lower wheel on this Bridgewood saw reveals the foot brake, brake pad, and integral micro-switch for quick blade braking and power shutoff.

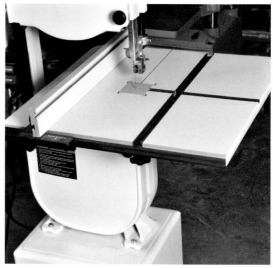

Auxiliary tables, such as this Rockler model, provide more work surface and include such amenities as T-tracks, circle-cutting jigs, adjustable fences, and replaceable throat inserts.

The single-point bar attached to this rip fence allows resawing of crooked or curved pieces.

This aftermarket fence from Laguna® Tools can be quickly adjusted to accommodate blade drift. It also includes a feed screw for accurate incremental fence positioning.

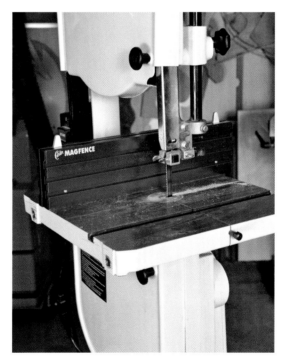

Rare earth magnets allow easy positioning of Carter's Magfence™ without the need for clamps or a fence rail.

Fences

Most new bandsaws come equipped with a basic proprietary rip fence. The angle on many of these fences can be adjusted to accommodate blade drift when ripping or resawing (see "Dealing with Drift" on p. 99). It's typically done by loosening the bolts that hold the fence rail to its clamping bar, setting the desired angle, and then locking down the bolts. Some fences include an attachable single-point bar to allow resawing crooked or curved lumber.

Aftermarket fences, which can be fit to various saws, are also available. Some feature easy-to-operate knobs for quick, accurate blade-drift adjustment. Some allow indexing for precise, repeatable fence positioning when resawing or ripping. Magnetically attachable fences allow positioning at any angle on an iron table without the need for a fence rail.

Of course, you can make your own bandsaw fence instead. A straight piece of wood clamped to the tabletop will serve as a no-frills version. Alternatively, you can make a more versatile fence by incorporating a bit of hardware, as shown on p. 119.

► QUICK TENSION-RELEASE RETROFIT

Although quick-release tension levers are becoming more prevalent on new bandsaws, you may have an older saw with only a tensioning knob. This requires lots of wrist aerobics every time you want to change a blade or release its tension on a saw that will sit idle for a while. To address this problem, Carter offers a conversion kit that will work with the majority of modern and older 14-in. cast-iron bandsaws. Simply called the Quick Release®, the accessory is easy to install and features two levels of release: The first simply relaxes the maximum tension for periods of disuse, while the second completely releases the tension for faster blade removal.

The saddle-shaped Quick Release lever easily installs on the upper frame of a cast-iron saw after the wheel house has been temporarily removed.

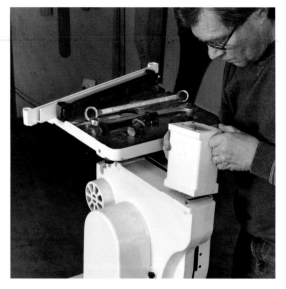

A 6-in.-high riser block kit will expand the resaw capacity of a two-piece cast-iron framed bandsaw.

Riser Block

Owing to the two-piece cast-iron frame of the typical 14-in. bandsaw, a hollow block of cast iron called a riser block can be placed between the two castings to effectively double the resaw capacity of the saw. The riser block kit includes a longer guidepost and a blade guard extension. The 6-in.-high riser block simply bolts between the two halves using the long replacement bolt supplied. Properly set up with an appropriate blade and a 1½-hp motor, a 14-in. machine like this can do a good job of resawing wide planks, although at a much slower feed speed than a big saw.

Mobile Base

Mobile bases typically have two non-swiveling casters and one or two swiveling casters. Lockable casters stabilize the machine in use. On some mobile bases, pedal-operated casters lift to allow that end of the base to drop to the floor on feet for stability.

MOBILE BASE OPTIONS

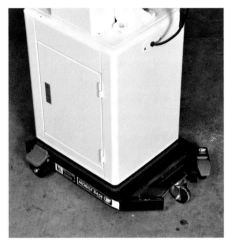

Custom-fit mobile bases, like the one at left, are available for specific saw models, while the universal version at center can be sized to fit a variety of saws. The universal kit at right involves attaching casters to a suitably sized plywood panel.

Manufacturers and aftermarket suppliers offer custom bases designed for specific saws or universal bases that will fit virtually any bandsaw. Mobile bases are relatively easy to build from scratch or from readily available kit parts. Make sure to use high-quality casters because bandsaws are heavy and will quickly destroy inexpensive versions.

[TIP] When positioning a bandsaw in a mobile base, locate the blade near the non-swiveling wheels to prevent machine movement due to feed forces.

Guides

The bandsaw accessories market is rife with replacement guides. Block guides made from ceramic or phenolic material are popular replacements for stock plastic or steel blocks. And if replacing the blocks doesn't seem adequate, the entire assemblies can be replaced with roller guides or purpose-designed ceramic guide assemblies. Aftermarket guides are often easier to adjust

A wide variety of aftermarket blade guides is available for virtually any make or model of bandsaw.

than the original stock guides and may lock more securely.

Anti-Fatigue Mat

An anti-fatigue mat improves comfort, safety, and performance at the bandsaw, where standing for long periods of time can

An anti-fatigue mat will reduce muscle strain during long sessions at the bandsaw. It also insulates feet against cold concrete floors.

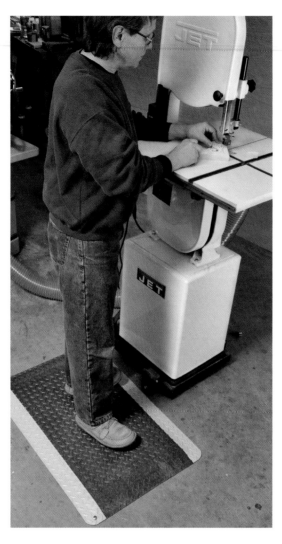

RHYMING , *CHEAP* AND *HEAP*

I have yet to find a really good new bandsaw at a bargain price—especially the typical 14-in. variety. Lots of brands look similar, but cheap saws typically have poorly machined castings, crooked guides, warped tables that flex, and a whole litany of problems that will be expensive to correct if they're even possible. Such flaws can reduce a bargain saw to an expensive boat anchor. Caveat emptor indeed.

be hard on your body. It will reduce muscle strain, helping you stay focused, and insulate your feet from a cold floor.

Buying New

Although good deals can be had buying used equipment, getting a new bandsaw has many advantages. But your success depends upon how well you identify your needs and how carefully you search out a saw that meets them. When buying new, you can choose the size of saw, its motor rating, and the types of accessories you need to suit the kind of work you do. As a bonus, you'll get a saw that is covered by a warranty and backed by a service department.

As you consider the purchase of a new saw, be realistic. A 20-in. bandsaw with a 5-hp motor might look regal sitting in your shop, but if you rarely rip lumber thicker than 6/4, cut heavy joinery, or resaw wide boards, you can forego that big of an investment. Instead, take the money you'll save by buying an appropriately sized saw and purchase an assortment of high-quality blades. You'll be better off.

Investigate the reputation of your chosen dealer, especially if you are buying online from a distant company. If you can't find information about it, contact one of the saw manufacturers to confirm that the dealer is authorized and in good standing. Ask the dealer about delivery costs and policies. If you lack means for unloading a heavy saw from a delivery truck, a lift-gate service can be specified but may cost extra. An additional freight charge may also apply to deliveries to a residential address.

Check warranty and return policies before buying. Most dealers will honor a manufacturer's warranty if a saw is defective. However, if you have to cover shipping costs to return the saw for repair or replacement, those costs may negate any advantage of buying out of town.

Target your needs using the checklist on p. 26. It will help prevent you from wasting hard-earned cash on a saw that is either overkill, too small, lacking in horsepower, or just too cheaply made to do the work you require. As you consider the list, here are some important points to consider.

Cutting Capacity

Two of your most important decisions involve a saw's *throat capacity* and its *resaw capacity*. The throat capacity is defined by the distance between the blade and the frame column, while the resaw capacity is the distance between the tabletop and the upper blade guides at their highest position. Sawing curves, especially tight scrolling, requires a wide throat but not much height, while resawing wide boards requires tall cutting capacity. If you only occasionally resaw lumber and typically use your saw for ripping or curve cutting, you really don't need 17 in. of resaw capacity and a 5-hp motor. You can efficiently resaw boards up to 5½ in. wide on a typical 14-in. bandsaw, which may be all you'll ever need.

Horsepower

If you plan on resawing stock wider than 6 in., you'll need at least a 1½-hp motor. And if you intend to rip a lot of heavy stock and resaw wide hardwood boards, buy as much horsepower as you can afford. Just make sure that your shop's electrical system can handle the load.

Large wing-head thumbscrews lock side and thrust guides in place while an indexing lock handle allows fore-and-aft adjustment of the entire guide assembly, providing tool-less guide adjustment.

Guides

Guides that securely hold their settings are crucial for accurate control of the blade. Make sure they have substantial mounts, are free of flex, and lock into place securely and easily, preferably without tools. Aftermarket guides can be purchased to replace inferior stock guides, but be sure to consider their expense in the overall cost of the saw. Sometimes upgrading to a saw with better stock guides saves money in the long term.

Table & Trunnions

In general, the larger the table, the better. A large table offers more work surface for better workpiece control, especially when scroll cutting. Look for table trunnions heavy enough to prevent the table from flexing

Use this form to compare new saw models and nail down the best saw for you.
Refer to the text for advice on the various features.

Dealer:

Brand: _____ model #: _____ serial #: _____

Price: _____ freight charges: _____

Wheel diameter: _____

Cutting capacity: _____ throat: _____ height: _____ max. blade width: _____

Horsepower: _____ voltage: _____

Guides: _____ block: _____ roller: _____

Frame material: _____ die-cast _____ cast iron _____ welded steel

Weight: _____

Table: _____ size: _____ miter slot? _____ T-slot?

_____ max. degree tilt to right: _____ max. degree tilt to left:

Trunnion material: _____ die-cast _____ cast iron _____ sheet steel

Dust collection: _____ number of ports: _____ diameter: _____

_____ located near the lower guide assembly? _____

_____ dust chamber in lower wheel house? _____

Warranty/Service: _____ warranty? _____ # of yrs. _____

_____ service department/technician available? _____

_____ spare parts available? _____

while secured at any angle. The trunnion lock should not slip, nor should it require excessive tightening.

Dust Collection

A large-diameter dust collection port close to the lower guide assembly is best. A partition surrounding the blade beneath the lower guides also helps concentrate the dust near the port. Dust ports at the bottom of the lower wheel housing are not particularly adept at collecting fine dust.

Buying Used

Great deals can be had on used bandsaws, although used machinery may require some work. Fortunately, bandsaw technology hasn't changed much in the past century, and it doesn't take an engineering degree to bring a good old horse back into harness. A used saw can be a gem or a stinker, though. It depends on its original quality, how well it was maintained, and whether it was modified in any way.

Keep in mind that many manufacturers no longer exist and that it can be difficult to locate replacement parts for an orphaned saw. If a used candidate is missing parts such as guides, tires, or bearings, check on their availability before buying. You may be able to substitute aftermarket parts or have parts fabricated, but maybe not.

Assessing an Old Saw

When assessing an old saw, bring along a few testing tools. Your kit should include a flashlight, a 2-ft. straightedge, a 6-ft. straightedge, various screwdrivers, some open-end wrenches, and a set of Allen

Heavy-duty trunnions and trunnion locks like these are stout enough to resist table deflection and maintain angle settings under moderate surface loads.

▶ SOURCES FOR OLD SAWS

I've found the best deals on used bandsaws through friends who know someone who knows someone with an old bandsaw in a shed. These "lost" saws are often in serviceable condition and very fairly priced. Keep your eyes open at garage sales and flea markets or when visiting other woodshops. Sometimes placing a want ad in a local paper can net a good deal. These days, the Internet offers sources such as Craigslist^{SM}, eBay^{SM}, and various woodworking sites that might include a classified-ad section. Even so, I look for saws that are relatively close to home, as I would never buy a used saw that I couldn't personally inspect, and shipping charges for a bandsaw can be prohibitively expensive.

When inspecting used saw candidates, here's a helpful checklist for reference and comparison purposes.

Seller:

Brand: model #:   serial #:

Wheel diameter:

Cutting capacity: throat: height: max. blade width:

Horsepower: voltage:

Guides: block: roller:

Upper guidepost flex?

Table: flat?   locks securely in place?

Cracked or welded frame?

Cracked or broken parts?

        wheels:

        wheel mount/tension mechanism:

        tension spring:

        trunnions:

Missing parts?

Tires: excessive wear?

Wheel bearings: quiet?   noisy?

        If Babbitt bearings, are they worn?

Wheel alignment: relatively coplaner?

Motor and drive: direct drive   belt driven   single phase   3 phase

Switch: operates properly?

Pulleys and belts: excessive wear?

Make test cuts. Comments:

wrenches. Make sure to perform the following tests on any saw before buying it (see chart at left).

Check for Guidepost Flex

The most important test of a used bandsaw is checking the upper guidepost for flex, especially in welded-steel bandsaws. Some early 1980s and 1990s consumer-grade welded-steel bandsaws lacked sufficient support for the upper guidepost, resulting in poor performance when resawing or cutting thick wood. To check, raise the upper guides about 6 in. off the tabletop. Apply moderate pressure from the front of the saw to mimic feed force, and look and feel for any flex. For heavy-duty cutting performance, the guides should be nearly immovable. Sometimes flex can be traced to an improper fit of the guidepost assembly to its support, which can often be cured by some judicious fine tuning. However, if the frame flexes, avoid the saw unless you plan to use it only for light work.

Inspect for Damage and Missing Parts

Look for cracks or welds in the frame, wheel support assemblies, and table support. A properly welded saw can still perform fine as long as accurate alignment of the parts has been maintained. If you aren't able to assess a good weld or can't measure the resulting alignment of parts, don't buy the saw.

Check for missing or damaged parts, especially in the upper wheel support/blade tension assembly. A broken tension spring can be easily replaced but indicates that the saw was misused. Any deformation of the axle/wheel support requires replacement of the parts. Defective guides can often be

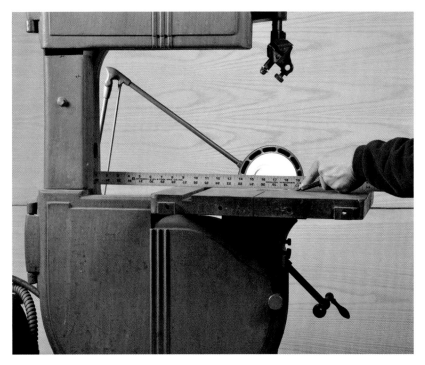

replaced easily with aftermarket guides, but the replacement cost should be factored into the purchase price.

Check the table for flatness with a good straightedge. Slightly warped tables can either be tolerated or machined true as long as the top is thick enough to allow it. Also inspect for cracks or repairs on the trunnions and their supports, and make sure the table doesn't flex when applying moderate downward pressure.

Check Tires & Wheels

If tires are worn or cracked, they can easily be replaced, but cracked or wobbly wheels are a serious problem. Sometimes replacement wheels can be located, but make sure they won't be too expensive. With the saw in tension, place your 6-ft. straightedge across the wheels to make sure they're not seriously misaligned. See p. 32 for further advice on the matter.

Use a good-quality straightedge and backlighting to quickly check for table flatness. An automotive feeler gauge can be used to measure any discrepancy.

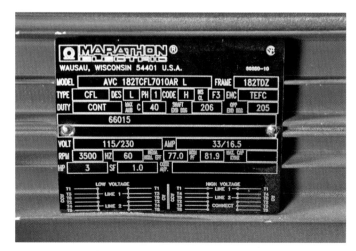

The phase of a motor is identified on its tag, preceded by the PH designation. The number 1 indicates single phase, compliant with standard 120/240-volt household current. A 3 indicates a three-phase motor, suited to 208–230/460 volts.

Remove the blade and drive belt if possible, and turn the wheels slowly by hand. They should be quiet. Noise indicates worn bearings that need replacement. Antique saws may have Babbitt bearings. Check them for wear, as they can be expensive to replace. Finally, note the condition of the pulleys and belts. Inexpensive die-cast pulleys can cause vibration, but they're easily replaced, as are stiff old V-belts.

Gauging Motor Power

A large, old single-phase motor, especially a repulsion-type motor, is sometimes hard to distinguish from a large, old three-phase motor. Three-phase motors are great when three-phase power is available because they're more efficient. However, if you don't have three-phase power in your shop, you'll have to invest in an expensive phase converter or change over to a single-phase motor (along with the necessary additional gearing). Some three-phase motors aren't easily replaced, especially if they directly drive the bottom wheel. To determine the phase, locate the identification tag on the motor and look for the letters "PH." They should be followed by either a "1" for single phase or a "3" for three phase.

Make Test Cuts

If the saw seems sound, make a few test cuts to really get a feel for the machine. Make sure that it doesn't bog down in thick material and that it tracks properly (keeping in mind that a dull, old blade may compromise the saw's operation). Make sure the machine doesn't vibrate excessively or squeal. If it does, try to locate the problem and see if it's correctable. If not, don't buy the saw.

Tune-Up
& Alignment

Tire Maintenance

➤ Recrowning Rubber
Tires (p. 50)

➤ Replacing Tires
(p. 51)

Handling Blades

➤ Folding a Bandsaw
Blade (p. 52)

Table Maintenance

➤ Making a Zero-
Clearance Insert
(p. 53)

A BANDSAW IS one of the most versatile tools in the woodshop. No other machine has the ability to rip, crosscut, and resaw, as well as cut curves and circles. Its thin, looped blade offers fast, efficient cutting using relatively low horsepower. It's great for shaping curves with perpendicular edges or compound edges used for sculptural work. You can also cut all sorts of joints with it.

However, to perform these tasks accurately the saw must be in proper adjustment and equipped with an appropriate blade for the task at hand. For accurate, efficient cutting, the wheels need to be outfitted with properly crowned tires and the blade guides must be accurately set to support the thin, flexible blade from the sides and rear.

Setting up the bandsaw is not difficult, but there are specific steps that must be taken in a certain order to wring optimum service from the tool. In this section I cover the entire range of setup and offer fixes for common problems such as blade vibration, wandering cuts, and resaw troubles.

Tools & Materials

You probably already have the common workshop tools needed for tuning your bandsaw. They include a good set of metric or ASE Allen wrenches, a high-quality square, a screwdriver or two, some open-end wrenches, and a pair of pliers. You'll also need a good-quality straightedge that's long enough to reach from the bottom rim of the lower wheel to the top rim of the upper

31

For tune-ups or blade changes, you'll need wrenches, screwdrivers, pliers, and an accurate square. The honing stone is used for rounding the back edge of the blade.

A cleaning and maintenance kit should include metal protectant, spray solvent, penetrating lubricant, paraffin, stiff bristle brushes, and sanding blocks (for crowning rubber tires).

wheel. A sharpening stone for rounding the backside of the blade completes the collection.

For general maintenance and to keep your bandsaw operating efficiently, you'll want a stiff bristle brush, spray solvent, spray lubricant, metal protectant, paraffin wax, and a wooden sanding block.

Machine Tune-Up

The bandsaw is a pretty simple machine in that it's basically comprised of two wheels that drive the blade, with blade guides to support the blade above and below the table. The machine includes wheel tracking and tensioning mechanisms and a motor to drive the wheels. Although it's not a terrifically complicated tool, all of its components must be working in concert to produce good cuts.

To make sure that your bandsaw is in good operating condition, you'll want to perform a few preliminary checks and adjustments. These include assessing the alignment of the wheels and drive pulleys, the condition of the tires and drive belts, and the adjustment of the table and guidepost. These particular tune-up steps won't have to be performed very often, but they are critical to successful operation.

Wheels

For a bandsaw to work at its best, the two wheels should ideally be coplanar (aligned in the same plane), concentric, and outfitted with tires that are slightly crowned. If the wheels are misaligned, the offset crowns may compete to steer the blade, causing tracking problems.

To check for coplanarity, begin by properly tensioning the largest blade that your saw is designed to handle. Then extend a straightedge fully across both wheels and tilt the upper wheel to be in parallel with the lower one. (Remember to re-track the

➤ See *"Mounting a New Blade"* on p. 41.

blade afterward.) To place the straightedge, you may have to remove the table or tilt it out of the way. If the straightedge contacts the upper and lower rim of both wheels at the same time, the alignment is fine. If the wheels are misaligned, you have the option of trying to adjust them. (However, you may not want to mess with this if your saw is tracking fine the way it is, as explained in the sidebar on p. 34.)

If your blade won't track properly, first investigate the simplest solutions, as explained on p. 46. If these don't correct

➤ See *"Blade Tracking"* on p. 46.

Tilting the table will often provide enough straightedge clearance to check the coplanarity of the wheels.

Wood extensions of identical width may be taped to a straightedge to allow clearance around a saw's frame. Groove the wood edges to house the straightedge.

COPLANARITY: THEORY VS. REALITY

For a bandsaw blade to track properly in the center of its wheels, the wheels should be *coplanar*, meaning in the same plane as each other. That's the theory, anyway. In the real world, you may discover that your saw's wheels are misaligned but that your blade is tracking very nicely. Furthermore, you may find that subsequent wheel alignment may cause the blade to track errantly. Go figure.

So, should you bring misaligned wheels into coplanarity? Not necessarily. Unless you're having blade tracking problems, you may want to leave well enough alone. I have worked with setups where the blade was tracking nicely on the upper wheel but running a bit off-center on the lower wheel and the saw still cut very accurately. Am I going to mess with that wheel alignment? Not a chance. I just thank the bandsaw gods and get back to work.

the problem, try aligning your wheels. Unfortunately, most owner's manuals don't address wheel alignment, and I couldn't hope to cover all possible machine configurations and corrections here. However, the drawing at right shows a basic approach for adjusting the upper wheel, which will work for many saws. A few bandsaw models include adjustment bolts on the lower wheel for easy alignment.

Out-of-round wheels/tires can cause *harmonic vibration* as the blade stretches and relaxes with each revolution around the wheels. This motion tends to work-harden the blade, which can induce breakage. Check

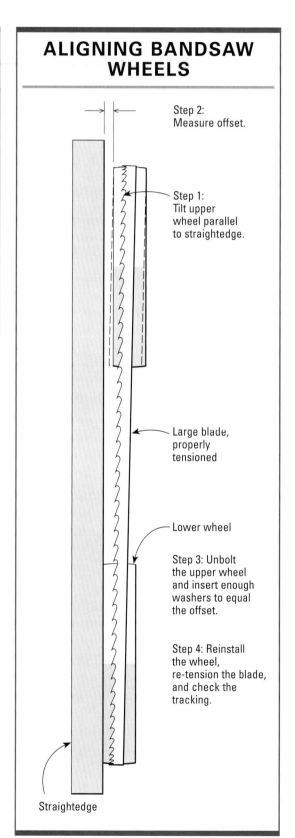

ALIGNING BANDSAW WHEELS

Step 2: Measure offset.

Step 1: Tilt upper wheel parallel to straightedge.

Large blade, properly tensioned

Lower wheel

Step 3: Unbolt the upper wheel and insert enough washers to equal the offset.

Step 4: Reinstall the wheel, re-tension the blade, and check the tracking.

Straightedge

Use a dial indicator mounted on a magnetic base to check the concentricity of wheels.

A few scraps of plywood can be quickly turned into a steady rest for "turning" the tires flat. Glue sandpaper to the rest with spray adhesive.

the tires for concentricity using a dial indicator with its magnetic base mounted to the saw table or cabinet. Place the indicator stylus against the center of the tire and slowly rotate the wheel. If eccentricity is excessive, you may want to remove the tire and check the wheel.

Eccentricity should not exceed 0.01 in. for 14-in. wheels, 0.012 in. for 18-in. wheels, and 0.015 in. for 20-in. wheels. If your wheels are badly out-of-round, a machine shop can true them. (Have wheels on new saws replaced under warranty.) If the tires are the culprit, they can be trued on the bandsaw using a sanding block and shop-made steady rest. Using a steady rest allows the sanding block to true the tire much like a tool rest on a lathe.

Tires

Fully tensioned saws that have sat unused for a while can develop an area of slight compression on each tire, which is caused by the unrelieved pressure of the blade. If the rubber is still in good shape, these flat spots may rebound after running the saw for a bit, erasing the problem. However, if the tires are time hardened, cracked, or excessively grooved, they should be replaced. Slightly grooved tires in otherwise good shape can be cleaned up and recrowned with sandpaper. A loose tire can simply be glued in place to prevent slipping.

► See *"Recrowning Rubber Tires"* and *"Replacing Tires"* on pp. 50–51.

Lay a straightedge across the faces of the pulleys to check for coplanar alignment.

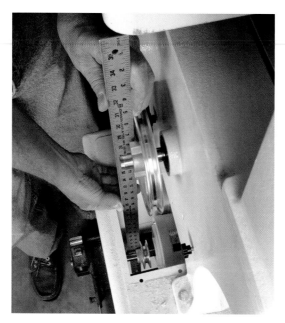

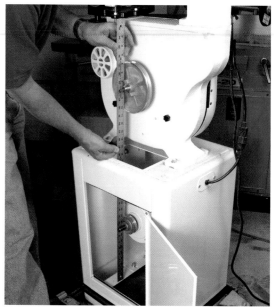

A segmented belt combined with machined pulleys can eliminate drive vibrations.

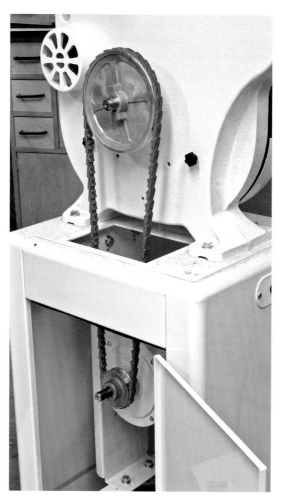

Drive Belts & Pulleys

A smoothly operating saw depends on well-aligned, good-quality pulleys outfitted with a pliable drive belt. To check that the pulleys are aligned, lay a straightedge across their faces. If they're misaligned, loosen the set screw on one of the pulleys and shift it into coplanarity with the other. Avoid moving the pulleys too far away from the bearing end of the shaft; the added leverage can stress the bearings, leading to premature failure.

Unfortunately, many saws come equipped with inexpensive die-cast metal pulleys that are often not truly concentric. This can cause the belt to gallop in the pulley grooves, transmitting vibration throughout the saw's frame. Add a cheap, stiff V-belt to the equation and you get a pulsing, buzzing irritant of a machine. Luckily, belt and pulley vibration is easy to correct by installing machined pulleys and/or a good-quality automotive-grade V-belt or segmented belt. (See Resources on p. 198.)

A multi-V belt drive provides good power transfer and low parasitic drag.

Recently, some tool manufacturers have started using multi-V belts on power tools. These thin, ribbed belts are very flexible and offer good power transfer with little parasitic drag. Multi-V belts require special pulleys and won't work with standard V-belt pulleys.

Table

The table on a bandsaw has the ability to tilt for cutting bevels and compound curves. The trunnions, which support the table, must be free of dirt, sawdust, and any other debris that may prevent the table from securely locking in position. The tabletop should be free of corrosion or crud that might prevent wood from sliding smoothly across the surface. I use a surface sealant such as Bostik TopCote® to keep the top slick.

[TIP] To prevent contaminating your project with finish-ruining silicone, use only silicone-free lubricant on your table.

Most bandsaw tables include a removable throat plate insert. Unfortunately, the slot in an insert tends to become enlarged over time due to inadvertent blade contact. A very narrow slot is best because it supports wood fibers on the underside of the workpiece, helping to minimize exit tearout and preventing small offcuts from jamming between the blade and wheel. The slot also helps stabilize the blade in the same fashion as the side guides. Replacement throat plates are available commercially, or you can make them yourself.

► See "Making a Zero-Clearance Insert" on p. 53.

A sharp blade that tracks correctly should cut perpendicular to the plane of the wheels—in other words, straight-on to the blade. Theoretically, that means that if the rip fence is square to the front of the table, and the table is square to the wheels, accurate fence-guided rips should result. On the other hand, a fence that's squared to a misaligned table can induce *blade drift*, which is the tendency of the blade to pull to one side or the other due to its nonparallelism with the fence. It's true that drift can also be caused by uneven blade wear, misadjusted guides, or improper blade tracking or tension, but squaring your table to the wheels at least eliminates any "built-in" blade drift caused by table misalignment. An accurately aligned table also aids cut accuracy when using a miter gauge or table slot-guided jig.

To check your table alignment, install the widest 3- or 4-tpi blade the saw will accept. Tension the blade and track it in the middle of the tire. Place a machinist's straightedge against the side of the blade, making sure it's touching the body of the blade—not a tooth. Compare the angle (if any) of the straight-

TABLE ALIGNMENT

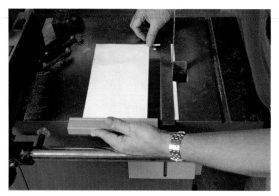 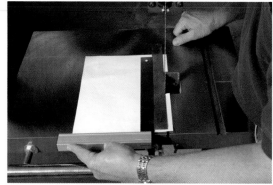

Using a sheet of paper to highlight any discrepancy, compare a straightedge aligned with the blade to a square placed against the front edge of the table. Loosening this table's mounting bolts allowed for shifting it into parallel with the straightedge.

Use an accurate try-square to set the table perpendicular to the blade.

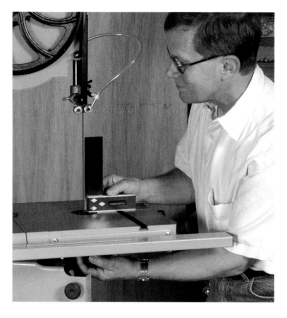

edge to a square placed against the front of the table or fence rail. If the alignment is only slightly off, you may be able to correct it by shifting the table a bit after loosening its mounting bolts. If the table requires more adjustment than the mounting holes allow, you can enlarge them with a file if you like.

Next, adjust the tilt of the table to square it to the sides of the blade. Most tables have an adjustable stop for easily resetting

the table to square after tilting it to make bevel cuts. Finally, "level" the table from front to back. That is, square it to the rear of the blade. This is particularly important for maintaining a square edge when cutting circles. The adjustment may require inserting shims between the table and its supporting trunnions.

Guidepost

The upper guidepost, which houses the upper blade guides, performs one of the saw's most critical functions: keeping the blade positioned properly during the cutting process. The guidepost should slide up and down easily and lock securely into position without using excessive force. If your saw is equipped with a rack-and-pinion system, make sure the gearing is lightly lubricated and free of sawdust. The guidepost itself should also be clean, corrosion-free, and lightly lubricated for smooth operation.

The primary job of the guidepost is to keep the upper blade guides aligned with their partners under the table. Misaligned guides—especially the thrust bearings—can

BEAM STRENGTH

A blade's beam strength provides its resistance to feed pressure, which tends to bow and twist the blade in use.

Feed pressure

Beam strength

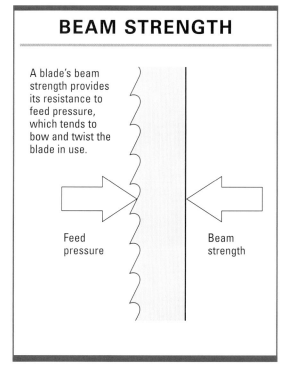

Use a dial indicator to check guidepost flex while resawing a board using moderate feed pressure.

cause the blade to twist, making for erratic cutting. Because it's so thin, a bandsaw blade relies on beam strength (the ability to resist bending along the length of the blade) to function. Properly aligned thrust bearings help provide that strength.

A few situations can shift the guidepost (along with its guides) out of alignment. One is flex. The post should not flex fore and aft or side-to-side when moderate pressure is applied to it. Guidepost flex can sometimes be cured by adjusting or hand-fitting the post and its housing components. Unfortunately, the flex can sometimes be caused by a twisting saw frame. This is more commonly a problem on saws with welded-steel frames. (Cast-iron frames have historically been more rigid.) That said, some manufacturers of welded-frame saws have increased rigidity in recent models, which are now on par with the best cast-iron-frame

saws. Regardless, the only way to prevent flex in a weak frame is to use very light feed pressure.

Another potential problem arises from a guidepost that doesn't stay perfectly aligned with the blade as it is repositioned at different heights. Some saws provide adjustments to align the guidepost. With others, you may have to do a bit of hand-fitting to bring the post into alignment. Often, though, the misalignment just has to be lived with by resetting the upper guides every time a major change is made in guide height position.

[TIP] If you plan to use your saw primarily for resawing or for sawing large bowl blanks, make sure the upper guidepost is absolutely without flex.

Changing Blades

The ability to change blades quickly and efficiently is one of the most valuable skills you can have at the bandsaw. Although it might seem complicated at first, once you

▶ BLADE CHANGE CHECKLIST

- Disconnect power.
- Move all blade guides away from blade.
- Release blade tension and remove blade.
- Clean tires and guides if necessary.
- Mount the new blade.
- Track and tension blade simultaneously.
- Move upper guide assembly to desired height.
- Set the thrust guides, then the side guides.
- Test cut.
- Recheck guides.

have changed blades a half-dozen times, it will get to be second nature. With practice and a good working knowledge of your bandsaw, you should be able to change blades, adjust the guides, and make a test cut or two in less than 10 minutes. Practice changing blades until the routine becomes familiar. It's time well spent.

In a nutshell, the sequence involves releasing the tension on the blade, removing it, mounting the replacement blade, re-tensioning and tracking it, and then aligning the blade guides. You may want to copy the checklist at left and tape it to your bandsaw until you become familiar with the process.

Removing the Old Blade

To remove the old blade, first disconnect the power, and then move the upper and lower side guides and thrust bearing far enough away from the blade to prevent interference during blade change and tracking. Also remove the table alignment pin from the end of the table slot.

Next, release the blade tension using the tension adjustment knob, wheel, or lever. Then slip the blade off of the tires and thread it through the table slot to remove it from the saw.

Clean and lubricate the thrust roller bearing guides. Although these are often sealed bearings, they can still lose their ability to move freely, so I frequently apply router bearing oil to them. European-style thrust and side bearings are not sealed and can wear quickly because they consist simply of a shaft running in a bushing. Therefore, I lubricate them frequently.

Before removing the old blade, retract the side guides and thrust bearing so they won't interfere when tracking the new blade.

To release the old blade, first back off the tension adjustment knob, wheel, or lever.

Also clean any accumulated sawdust off the tires with a stiff nylon- or brass-bristle brush. Take care to not damage the tires with overenthusiastic cleaning. While you're at it, get in the habit of quickly checking for cracks or grooves in the tires.

Mounting a New Blade

Install the blade on the upper wheel first, making sure that the teeth point downward toward the saw table. (If they point in the opposite direction, simply grasp the blade and turn it inside out.) Use a spring clamp to secure the blade to the upper wheel while slipping it over the lower wheel.

Apply enough tension to take the slack out of the blade, and then slowly turn the upper wheel by hand while alternately tracking and tensioning the blade. Do not fully tension the blade until it is tracking exactly in the center of the tire, as you can't properly tension a roving blade.

> ⚠ **WARNING** **Never tension the blade with the saw running.**

Clean debris from tires using a stiff nylon- or brass-bristle brush.

Use a spring clamp to secure the blade to the upper wheel while slipping the opposite end of the loop onto the lower wheel.

Simultaneously tension and track the blade while rotating the upper wheel by hand.

A properly tensioned blade should deflect about ¼ in. under moderate finger pressure.

▶ BLADE TENSIONING SPRING

A bandsaw tension spring can fail without showing any breakage. If the spring has been stressed past its rating, the intergranular structure of its steel can disintegrate, causing the spring to lose its ability to hold tension. Also, a compression spring should never be squeezed beyond approximately 85% of its stroke—the stroke representing the difference between the length of the spring at rest and its length when completely compressed. Compressing the spring completely can result in premature spring failure, regardless of any outward physical signs.

Completely compressing a tension spring as shown here can result in premature spring failure.

Bump the on/off switch briefly and check the tracking as the motor coasts down. Adjust it if necessary, turning the wheel by hand. After the blade is tracking correctly, lock the tracking knob, close the wheel house doors, start the saw, and let it run at full speed for a few seconds. Then bring the blade up to final tension (according to the tension gauge) and run the saw again for a few seconds to make sure the tracking stays true.

The tension gauges on most bandsaws are accurate enough for this initial tension setting. However, it's wise to double-check the tension using a different approach, since a number of things can compromise the gauge's accuracy, including a heavy-duty replacement spring. Fully raise the guide-post, and then push against the side of the blade using moderate pressure. (If your saw is equipped with a tension release lever, make sure it is engaged in the full tension position.) Fine-tune the blade's tension so that it deflects about ¼ in.

Follow up by making a few cuts in scrap that is the same thickness and density as your intended workpiece. If necessary, the blade's performance can often be improved by increasing or decreasing the tension.

▶ See *"Troubleshooting"* on p. 45.

⚠ **WARNING Never fully compress the tension spring, which can result in catastrophic damage to the upper wheel mount assembly.**

▶ TENSION GAUGES

Proper blade tension is crucial to accurate sawing. Insufficient tension can cause blade wander, but unnecessarily high tension is hard on tires and can cause blade breakage and catastrophic failure of bandsaw parts. However, don't trust your bandsaw's tension gauge to provide the exact tension your blade requires. Use it instead to get you in the neighborhood. Too many variables can compromise an accurate reading, including the blade's thickness, hardness, pitch, and manufacturing process. The "correct" tension is simply that which causes the blade to perform at its best.

Some blade manufacturers recommend very specific tension ratings, which vary from brand to brand and blade to blade. Commercial tension gauges are available that will provide readings in pounds per square inch, but they're very pricey, and I consider them overkill for wood-cutting bandsaws smaller than 24 in.

So what's my approach? I simply gauge the amount of sideways deflection of a fully exposed blade and then assess the cutting action using scrap, as explained under "Mounting a New Blade" on p. 41.

High-quality precision tension gauges are accurate but very expensive.

Setting the Blade Guides

The first item to address when setting the guides is whether the guide holder is square to the blade. If the bearing surfaces of the side guides—whether rollers or blocks—aren't parallel to the blade, it will be inadequately supported, possibly inducing an erratic cut.

To check your saw, first install a blade that is wider than the guide surface and locate the guides close to the blade. Check for a consistent gap between the blade and each guide. (It's a good idea to square the faces of block guides before checking this.) If the faces of block guides or the edges of roller guides aren't parallel to the blade, you can try rotating the guide assembly on the post to correct the problem. Loosen the guide holder just enough to allow movement, pinch the blade between the side guides, lock them in place, and then tighten the guide holder. This should square everything up.

This misaligned guide assembly (near right) causes the side guides to be out of parallel to the blade. In the photo at far right, the guide assembly has been rotated on the guidepost to bring the guides into parallel with the blade.

If a poorly machined guide holder won't allow setting for parallelism, you may have to perform some corrective machining on your saw. Alternatively, if you're using block guides, their faces can be surfaced at a slight angle to parallel the blade.

> See *"Squaring Block Guides"* on p. 80.

Set the guidepost to accommodate the height of the workpiece, and then position the upper and lower side guide assemblies to set the guides slightly behind the back edge of the blade gullets. Now you're ready to adjust the thrust bearings and side guides to support the blade.

Set the thrust guides first. Ceramic guides and roller bearing guides can be positioned to lightly touch the blade. However, it's also fine to set them a few thousandths of an inch away, as long as the space is equal on both guides. A dollar bill or a piece of a brown grocery bag is the age-old standard for spacing the guides. Wrap the paper around the blade and carefully set the guides snug to the paper without moving the blade

as the guides are tightened. Setting the upper and lower thrust guides precisely equidistant from the back edge of the blade is critical to preventing blade twist, especially when resawing and cutting other thick stock.

Next, adjust the side guides. Ceramic, phenolic, and perimeter-contact roller bearing guides can be set to lightly touch the blade. Wood, metal, and face-contact roller bearing guides should be spaced a dollar bill's thickness away from the blade. In the case of very narrow blades, it's best to trap them within wood or phenolic side guides or to use a specialty guide that provides thrust and side control for narrow blades.

> See *"Blade Guides"* on p. 68.

[TIP] If a faulty guidepost won't adjust parallel to the blade, reset your guides whenever you change the guidepost height to accommodate a different stock thickness.

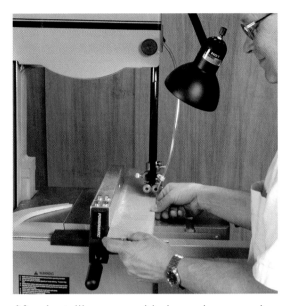

After installing a new blade, make several straight and curved test cuts to ensure that the blade tracks and cuts accurately.

Testing the Tune-Up

When installing a blade, new or used, it's wise to make a couple of curved and straight test cuts to see how well the machine cuts before committing to your project wood. If the cut wanders, recheck the guides. If the blade vibrates or bows, its tension is probably insufficient. If the guides are set correctly and the tension is adequate but the cut still wanders, a worn blade is most likely the culprit. In that case, it's best to switch over to a new blade.

[TIP] A sharp blade that is appropriate for the sawing task at hand is essential for maintaining a bandsaw's performance.

Troubleshooting

Working with a bandsaw that's cutting incorrectly can be frustrating, but a bit of detective work can usually solve the problem.

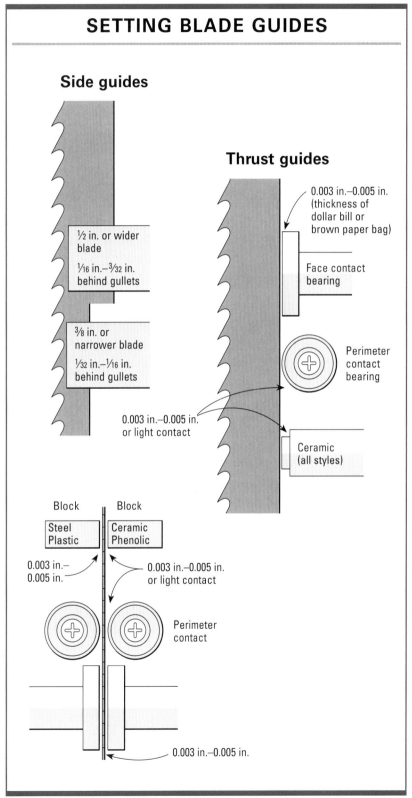

SETTING BLADE GUIDES

Side guides

½ in. or wider blade
¹⁄₁₆ in.–³⁄₃₂ in. behind gullets

³⁄₈ in. or narrower blade
¹⁄₃₂ in.–¹⁄₁₆ in. behind gullets

0.003 in.–0.005 in. or light contact

Thrust guides

0.003 in.–0.005 in. (thickness of dollar bill or brown paper bag)

Face contact bearing

Perimeter contact bearing

Ceramic (all styles)

Block — Steel Plastic
Block — Ceramic Phenolic

0.003 in.–0.005 in.

0.003 in.–0.005 in. or light contact

Perimeter contact

0.003 in.–0.005 in.

The most common issues involve vibration, bowed cuts, blowout, blade wander, and binding or burning. Not to worry, though. Each of these problems has a cure.

Blade Tracking

A blade that wanders off track or that won't stay centered on the upper wheel can cause serious cutting problems and may even result in the blade coming off the tires. Causes may include insufficient blade tension, inaccurate tire crowns, non-coplanar wheels, or a combination of the three.

To solve the problem, begin with the easiest approaches and work backward. First check the blade tension (after retracting the thrust bearings so they don't interfere). If necessary, readjust it while tracking the blade until sufficient tension is achieved with the blade tracking in the center of the tire. Be careful not to over-tension the blade. If that doesn't correct the tracking, inspect your tire crowns. If they are very worn, recrown them or replace the tires. If the blade still won't track properly, make sure your wheels are coplanar and correct the alignment if necessary.

▶ See *"Recrowning Rubber Tires"* and *"Replacing Tires"* on pp. 50–51.

▶ See *"Aligning Bandsaw Wheels"* on p. 34.

Vibration or Rippled Cut

Sometimes a particular chance combination of blade tension and feed rate can cause harmonic blade vibration that creates a rippled cut. Changing the tension or feed rate somewhat will usually eliminate the

An unlucky combination of blade tension and feed rate can cause a rippled cut like this one.

problem. Switching to a variable-pitch blade (designed to help eliminate vibration) can also help eliminate the problem.

Bowed or Bellied Cut

Inadequate blade tension can cause a bowed or bellied cut in thick stock. Blades with too fine a pitch (too many teeth) for the material thickness can also cause bowing, especially if the feed rate is too quick. Dull blades can really cause problems due to the extreme feed pressure needed to make the cut. The bowing usually becomes more severe as the cut progresses, resulting in binding, high blade temperatures, and the possibility of blade breakage.

When experiencing bowing, first ensure that you have an appropriate blade installed and that it is reasonably sharp. Next, try increasing the blade tension or slowing the

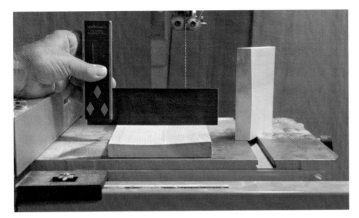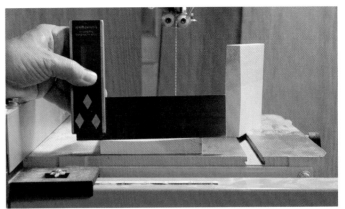

An insufficiently tensioned blade caused this bowed cut, which starts straight and square (left) but then bellies out after only 5 in. (right).

feed rate, or both. (But don't overdo the tension, which could damage the blade or the saw.)

[TIP] **To back a blade out of a bowed cut, wedge the leading edge open enough to extricate the blade.**

Blowout

Blowout occurs during resawing, when a blade breaks through the side of the workpiece. The problem is a result of the upper and lower thrust bearings not being coplanar to each other. As the blade is pressed against one bearing initially, and then the other, it's forced to twist in response. And once the errant cut is started, the blade tends toward that direction, whether toward the fence or away from it. The blowout often occurs near the bottom of the cut, particularly on saws whose lower guides are some distance from the table.

To prevent blowout, make sure your upper and lower thrust bearings are coplanar. Also, use as wide a blade as possible. This problem is less common on saws with stronger

Non-coplanar thrust guides caused by poor adjustment or guidepost flex can cause blowout at the bottom of a cut.

frames, which help prevent guidepost movement. If you find that your guidepost is flexing, slow your feed rate to minimize the pressure against the blade.

Wandering

The tendency of a blade to wander from the cut line is often caused by side guides set too far away from the blade. A dull blade can also cause wandering due to the increased feed force needed to push the wood against the blade. Excessive feed pressure can force the blade to twist slightly, resulting in a cut that wanders side to side. To minimize or prevent the problem, adjust wood, ceramic, roller bearing, or phenolic guides very close to the blade—even lightly touching it. And again, make sure your blade is sharp and appropriate for the task.

Burning or Binding

Burning or binding in a curved cut is usually the result of using too wide a blade for the cut radius. Switching to a narrower blade should correct the problem. It also helps to round the back edge of a new blade, as shown in "Stoning a Blade" on the facing page. Sometimes, poorly seasoned lumber or internally stressed "reaction wood" can pinch the blade during cutting. No problem—just push a small wooden wedge into the cut to relieve the squeeze.

The burned wood and bowed cut here are caused by using too wide a blade for the radius being sawn.

Blade binding in a cut can be eliminated by inserting a wedge into the cut.

General Maintenance

As with any machine, a bandsaw requires occasional cleaning and lubrication to operate well. The tires should be kept free of built-up sawdust, the bearings need lubrication, the table should be kept clean and corrosion-free, and certain types of guides need occasional truing.

Cleaning

Bandsaw tires must be kept relatively clean to ensure proper tracking and traction. Built-up sawdust can effectively change the crown of the tire, causing errant blade tracking. It can also cause vibration by creating a "rough road" for the blade to travel on. Furthermore, excessive debris can impede the traction necessary to power the blade through its cut.

Some bandsaws come equipped with a stiff brush that's mounted in the lower wheel housing. It continually rides against the tire to clean off sawdust. The upper wheel stays relatively clean because most of the sawdust falls into the lower wheelhouse. To clean tires, I use a household brush with stiff nylon bristles. A brass-bristle brush works well, too, but avoid steel-bristle brushes, which can damage the tires. To remove heavily encrusted crud, I use a sanding block, wielding it with a light enough touch to clear away only the debris.

Dirty or rusty saw tables can impede stock feeding and cause inaccurate cuts, especially when sawing curves freehand. I use a good spray solvent to clean away the coating of old metal protectant as well as any pitch or gummy detritus. I follow up by scrubbing off any remaining rust or crud using steel wool, a Scotch-Brite™ pad, or 600-grit sandpaper.

A stiff-bristle brush mounted in the lower wheel house helps clear sawdust off the tire.

After one final quick cleaning with the solvent, I apply a couple of light coats of tabletop protectant, wiping off the excess after each coat.

Truing Guide Blocks

Guide blocks are subjected to nearly constant contact with the blade. This friction will often produce uneven wear and a notched or angled face on the block. An easy fix is to sand the face flat, which restores its ability to offer full blade support. (Ceramic guides can be trued on a diamond sharpening stone.) Note that some guide block holders are not cast or machined true and that the face of the guide may have to be shaped to a slight bevel to create parallelism with the blade.

STONING A BLADE

When cutting curves, the sharp corners on the rear of the blade can scrape against the side of the kerf, contributing to balky feeding. The sharp edges can also bite into thrust bearings, inviting grooving. Because of this, it's a good idea to ease the back edges of a new blade with a honing stone to make it glide more smoothly through curves and protect against bearing wear. Stoning a blade also removes any rough areas or misalignment near the blade weld.

You can buy special stones for the purpose at many woodworking supply stores, or you can simply use a regular sharpening stone. With the saw running, rest the stone on the table and press it against the rear of the blade while rotating the stone around the rear edge. This will ease the corners into a more rounded shape. Don't apply so much pressure that you push the blade off the tires. Be patient. The process will take about five minutes. The stoning will create sparks, so be sure to first remove any sawdust accumulation inside the saw.

Resting a honing stone on the saw table, rotate it from side-to-side around the back of a running blade to ease the rear edges.

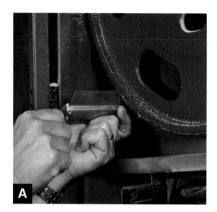
A

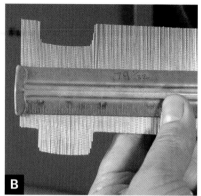
B

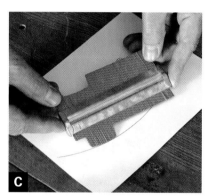
C

D

E

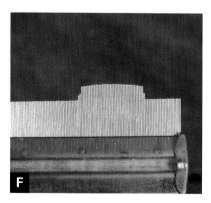
F

Recrowning Rubber Tires

As bandsaw tires wear, they lose the crown that keeps the blade tracking correctly. Tires also can become grooved from blade teeth, and they may retain embedded sawdust that even a good brushing won't remove. Fortunately, it's easy to renew the crown on rubber tires while cleaning up the grooves and detritus in the process. All it takes is a wood block faced with 100-grit sand-paper, a profile gauge, a compass, and a few minutes.

[TIP] Urethane tires are more durable than rubber tires, but they're more difficult to recrown. Simply replace them when worn.

The crown on a bandsaw tire is often hard to dis-cern because the wheel housing or other obsta-cles obstruct the view. To read the initial shape of the crown, I push a profile gauge against the tire **(A)** and **(B)**. If the original crown has been extremely flattened or grooved, I create a 6-in. radius on card stock, which I then use as a com-parison reference for my profile gauge **(C)**.

With the saw unplugged, turn the wheel by hand and sand the profile on the tire. Check your prog-ress frequently with the profile gauge. Sand just enough to renew the crown **(D)** while removing any grooves **(E)**. Measure inward from the wheel rim to make sure the crown is centered on the tire. A reading taken with your profile gauge will tell you when you've reached the right shape **(F)**.

Replacing Tires

A new set of tires isn't hard to install using a few clamps, a bench vise, and some solvent **(A)**. Remove the old tire by prying it off the rim with a small pry bar. If it is securely glued to the wheel, lift an area, slice the tire, and then peel it off the rim **(B)**. Clean the wheels with solvent to remove old glue or grime. A final cleaning with alcohol will remove any solvent residue **(C)**.

[TIP] The lower wheel on a bandsaw is held on with a left-hand threaded bolt or nut.

Soak the replacement tires in hot water for a few minutes to make them more pliable **(D)**. Quickly wipe the tire dry before stretching it over the wheel. Slip the tire over the lower half of the wheel, and secure the wheel in a bench vise. With spring clamps holding the lower half of the tire in place, stretch the remaining half over the rim **(E)**.

Urethane tires don't need to be glued to the rim unless they are slightly oversized or have stretched a bit too much during installation. Being very thin, they are not prone to bunching up from blade pressure and won't "crawl" around the rim like a thicker rubber or neoprene tire might. If a urethane tire needs to be glued to the rim to prevent crawling, use a two-part epoxy to assure an adequate bond to the urethane.

Rubber or neoprene tires should be glued on. Several bandsaw tire suppliers offer special adhesives for the job, but I find that 3M™ Fast Tack trim adhesive (available at auto supply stores) works just as well. Slip a large-diameter bolt, wood dowel, or pipe under the tire to hold it away from the wheel while you apply the glue underneath. Work completely around the wheel in this fashion **(F)**.

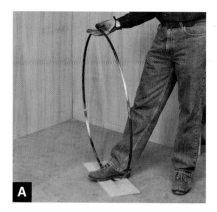
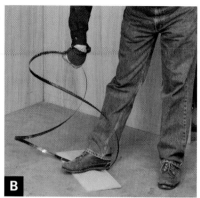
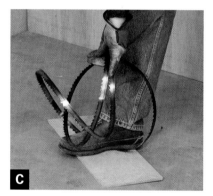

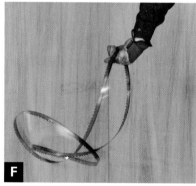
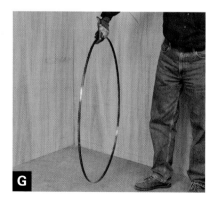

Folding a Bandsaw Blade

Bandsaw blades are typically "folded" into three coils for easy handling and storage. Although this can be done with just two hands, I prefer the more controlled technique of stepping on one end of the blade while rotating it into a coil with my hand. This method is safe for both large and small blades and eliminates the danger of the blade flipping back toward you during the process. Always wear heavy leather gloves when coiling or uncoiling a bandsaw blade.

To fold a blade, begin by holding it in your hand with the teeth pointing away from you **(A)**. Twist the blade 180° in a counterclockwise rotation **(B)**. Keep twisting to a complete a 360° rotation, lowering the blade toward the floor as you go **(C)**. Then gather the three coils together **(D)**. To prevent the blade from springing open, give it a quick wrap with a piece of masking tape or wire.

[TIP] To prevent blade tooth damage from a concrete floor, place the blade on a piece of scrap wood.

To uncoil a blade, hold it with the teeth facing away from you. With your forefinger, separate one coil, holding it between your thumb and forefinger **(E)**. Lightly grasping the separated coil between your thumb and the base of your forefinger, toss the blade away from you with a counterclockwise twist of your wrist **(F)**. The blade will want to twist in your hand, so maintain a controlled but responsive grip on it, allowing it to pivot as needed without letting it fly. The uncoiled blade is now ready for installation **(G)**.

Making a Zero-Clearance Insert

Resaw a piece of tight-grained hardwood, such as maple or cherry, to a slightly thicker dimension than the original throat plate. I measure the thickness using a dial caliper **(A)**. Use a compass to scribe the exact diameter of the original insert, and then rough cut the circle, staying slightly outside the line. Follow up by cutting exactly to the line **(B)**. Check the diameter against the original insert, or, if you care to remove the saw blade, fit the insert blank to the throat opening of the table. If your bandsaw has a registration pin in the insert opening, cut a notch in the new insert, orienting the grain crosswise to the front of the table.

Before cutting the slot, first measure the distance from the front of the throat opening to the front edge of the blade **(C)**. Mark this distance on the insert blank. Set the rip fence exactly adjacent to the edge of the throat opening, and use it to guide the new throat plate while cutting the slot **(D)**. This accurately locates the slot, even if the blade is off-center to the opening. Making the cut perpendicular to the grain prevents the insert from splitting into two pieces along the slot line.

Perform any necessary final trimming to fit the insert into its opening. If it's a bit too thick, trim it flush to the table surface with a block plane **(E)** or sanding block (after removing the blade). If it's a bit too thin, shim it up at the edges with masking tape. (The insert needs to be flush around the entire circumference because the work often pivots around the blade and can get hung up on any slight edge.) Apply a light coat of wax, and you're ready to go **(F)**.

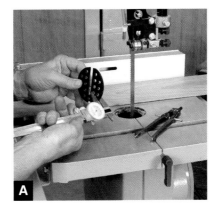
A

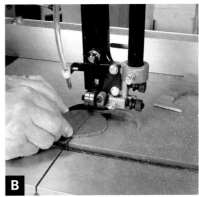
B

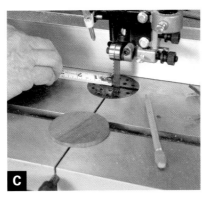
C

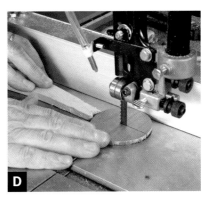
D

E

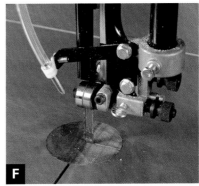
F

Bandsaw Blades

The essence of a bandsaw is in its blade. This thin, narrow strip of steel forms an endless loop with a cutting edge of teeth that are punched out, ground to shape, or attached. A bandsaw blade needs to be flexible enough to easily rotate around the wheels while still maintaining enough resistance against feed forces to avoid deflection or twisting during the cut.

There are dozens of blade configurations available, and proper selection is important because the right blade can make your bandsaw sing, while the wrong one will make you scream in frustration. The blade's width, pitch (teeth per inch), tooth configuration, and type of metal are all interdependent. Selecting the right blade for the job can seem daunting, but it's relatively simple once you understand a bit about blade technology and terminology.

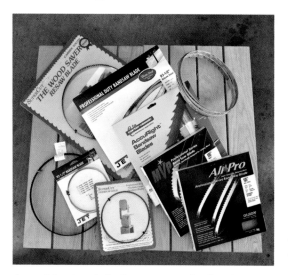

A multitude of choices can make buying the correct bandsaw blade a real challenge.

In this section you will learn how to put together a complement of blades that will suit your woodworking needs. You'll find that a few well-chosen blades will easily outperform and outlast inappropriate blades that strain to execute tasks they weren't intended to fulfill.

Blade Terminology

Knowing the terms associated with bandsaw blade construction makes it easier to assess the correct blade for your needs. It also gives you a common frame of reference with your blade dealer when discussing or ordering blades with specific characteristics. The drawing on the facing page shows all of the parts of the blade and the names for them.

Blade Material

Various types of steel are used to make bandsaw blades, offering you a range of choices based on economy, durability, or a compromise between the two. It helps here to understand just a few basics about bandsaw metallurgy: There are two main classes of steel: carbon steel and alloy steel. Carbon is added to steel to make it harder. Alloy steel—also referred to as spring steel—is carbon steel alloyed with another metal, such as chromium, silicon, tungsten, vanadium, molybdenum, or cobalt, to increase its strength and/or heat resistance. Heat-treating alloyed carbon steel produces high-speed steel.

Carbon Steel

Carbon is the element that turns iron into steel. The higher the carbon content, the harder the steel. Many blades are made entirely from high-carbon steel, with their teeth punched or cut into the edge of the band. These offer an economical alternative to blades with more durable high-speed steel or carbide teeth. And they're available in a wide variety of sizes and tooth configurations.

Some carbon steel blades are edge-hardened using flame or induction heating (an electrical current process) to increase the hardness of the teeth and/or back. This gives them enough strength and abrasion resistance to perform well as general-purpose blades in a typical woodworking shop. In fact, a carbon steel blade that is appropriate for the task at hand might even last longer than a higher-quality blade that is being forced to perform duties for which it's ill suited.

Spring Steel

Spring steel is any carbon steel that has been alloyed with another metal. Spring-steel blades have gotten a somewhat undeserved reputation for poor quality because of many low-cost versions on the market. Made from low-carbon steel alloys with unhardened die-cut teeth, these cheap blades are really only suited for softwood or thin hardwood. However, high-quality spring-steel blades are also available, made from harder high-carbon steel alloyed with additives such as manganese to further increase strength. Some are also heat-hardened for greater durability and abrasion resistance.

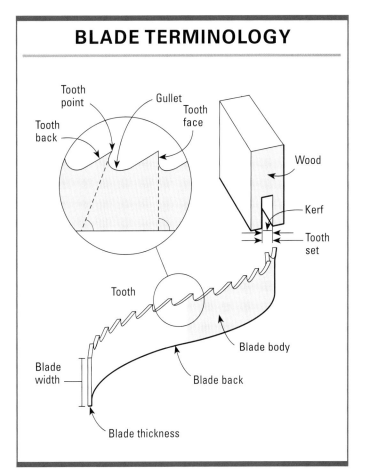

BLADE TERMINOLOGY

Tooth point · Gullet · Tooth face · Tooth back · Wood · Kerf · Tooth set · Tooth · Blade body · Blade width · Blade back · Blade thickness

High-Silicon Steel

High-silicon steel is often referred to as "Swedish silicon steel," although it's actually produced worldwide. With a silicon content tenfold that of conventional spring steel, these blades offer superior heat resistance, which is why metal-cutting blades are commonly made from high-silicon steel. However, high silicon content does not greatly increase the steel's abrasion resistance, which is more important than heat resistance when cutting wood.

▶ HEAT-TREATED BLADES

As part of the manufacturing process, some blades undergo heat treatment by flame or electrical induction to harden the metal. A blade with hardened teeth is called a *hard edge* blade. By contrast, a *hard back* blade is one whose back edge has been heat-hardened to resist "mushrooming" caused by aggressive contact with thrust bearings during heavy cutting.

The darkened edges on this blade show evidence of heat treatment. Because both the teeth and rear edge have been heat-hardened, this is called a *hard edge/hard back* blade.

BIMETAL BLADE

On a bimetal blade, the tooth tips that remain from an attached strip of high-speed steel create a very durable cutting edge.

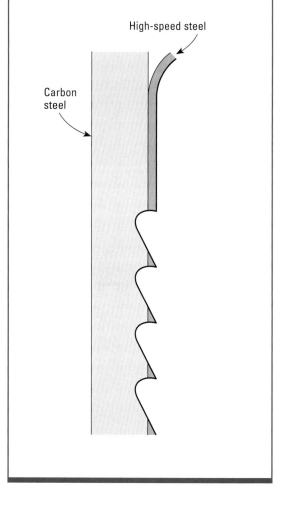

High-speed steel

Carbon steel

Bimetal

A bimetal blade is constructed by welding a narrow strip of high-speed steel (typically M2) to the front edge of a carbon steel blade body. The gullets are cut into the front edge, leaving very durable tooth tips on a flexible-bodied blade. The back edges of some bimetal blades are hardened to resist heavy pressure against the thrust bearings, especially during resawing.

CARBIDE BLADE

Individual carbide teeth welded to a flexible blade body provide the ultimate in cutting durability.

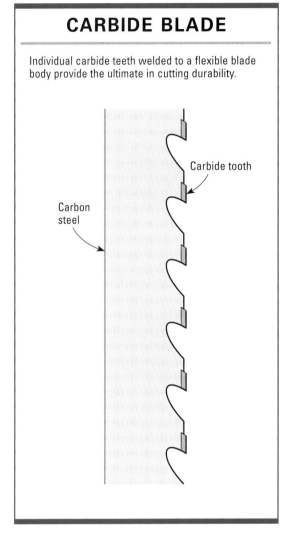

Carbide tooth

Carbon steel

CARBIDE-IMPREGNATED BLADE

Tiny carbide particles are electrically injected by a cathode to create hardened teeth.

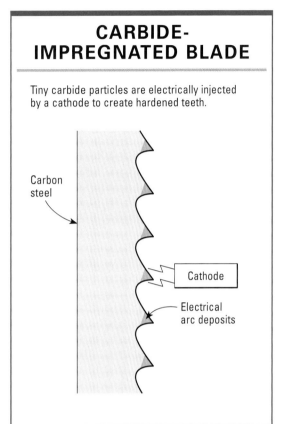

Carbon steel

Cathode

Electrical arc deposits

Carbide Tooth

Carbide, a tungsten-carbon alloy, is very dense and hard. Individual carbide teeth are welded to a spring steel body to create a blade with an exceptionally long-lasting cutting edge. Carbide grades range from C1 through C8. The lower the number, the tougher and more impact resistant the carbide. The higher the number, the harder and more abrasion resistant it is. For woodworking, abrasion resistance is more important than impact resistance, so a higher number is better.

Carbide-Impregnated Steel

Carbide-impregnated blades are created by electrically depositing tiny particles of titanium carbide onto the blade's teeth, in effect face-hardening the high-carbon steel teeth. The particles displace carbon steel particles and actually become an integral part of the steel, providing good abrasion resistance.

[TIP] Many exotic woods, such as teak, contain very abrasive silica. Bimetal or carbide blades will withstand the abrasion much better than standard carbon or spring steel.

Tooth Manufacture

There are three basic approaches to manufacturing bandsaw blade teeth. The first—usually associated with lower-cost blades—is to punch them out of the edge using a die.

ROCKWELL HARDNESS

Most blade manufacturers quote figures for the Rockwell hardness of a blade's teeth, and often for its body as well. The designation is stated as *Rc* followed by a number. The higher the number, the harder the metal. The rating isn't necessarily an indication of abrasion resistance but simply states how hard the steel has become through alloying and heat treating.

TEETH PER INCH (tpi)

To determine the tpi, or pitch, of a blade, measure point to point over 1 in., and then count the gullets in between.

|← 1 in. →|
|← 4 tpi →|

1 2 3 4

Sometimes this is followed up by grinding, but often not, and the punched teeth can suffer from random quality and sharpness. The second method is to gang the blades together much like the stacked plates in a laminated padlock, and then mill the shape of the teeth across all of the blades at once. The third method is to machine blades one at a time, a more intensive manufacturing process but often representative of a better-quality blade.

Pitch

Pitch refers to the number of teeth per inch (tpi) on a bandsaw blade. Blades are available in 2-, 3-, 4-, 6-, 8-, 10-, 14-, 18-, 24-, and 32-tooth configurations. The number of teeth correlates to the tooth type and blade width. Higher-pitch blades (having more teeth) cut smoother but slower. Low-pitch blades (with fewer teeth) have larger gullets, which evacuate sawdust more efficiently to allow a faster, although rougher, cut. As a general rule, at least three teeth should be in the workpiece to prevent excessive vibration and rough cuts.

Variable-pitch blades combine different tpi configurations to reduce blade flutter caused by harmonic vibration. For example, the teeth might alternate between 2 tpi and 3 tpi along the length of the blade. Variable-pitch blades are particularly useful when resawing thick lumber.

Tooth Shape

Choosing a blade with the correct tooth shape is critical to good performance and quality of cut. A combination of an aggressive hook-tooth profile with few teeth per inch and large gullets will cut very efficiently, but with a rough finish. A regular-tooth blade with many teeth per inch will cut smoothly, but the small gullets will strain mightily trying to remove the sawdust while cutting thick wood. Understanding how different tooth shapes work and how best to apply them will result in better cuts, longer blade life, and a lot less frustration.

Regular Tooth

Regular-tooth blades have evenly spaced teeth with a 0° rake angle, which creates a scraping cut. Considered general-purpose blades, they offer a smooth, precise cut for crosscuts, ripping of thin stock, and contour sawing. Because of the 0° rake angle and small gullets, these blades are not especially suitable for resawing, and cutting curves in thick lumber will require slow feed rates to allow chip evacuation. Regular blades typically have a raker tooth set and are available in widths of ⅛ in., ³⁄₁₆ in., and ¼ in.

Skip Tooth

Skip-tooth blades have longer gullets between the teeth because every other tooth is essentially "skipped," or omitted. When compared to a hook-tooth blade, a skip-tooth blade has proportionately smaller teeth for the length of the gullet between them. With a 0° rake angle and large gullets, this type of blade can evacuate large quantities of sawdust. It is fast-cutting and well suited for resinous softwoods, whose sticky sawdust can be problematic. This type of tooth won't crosscut as cleanly as a regular tooth and can't compete with a hook-tooth blade for resawing, but it is a good compromise for curved work, which involves both crosscutting and ripping.

tpi and Material Thickness

The fewer teeth per inch on a blade, the faster (but rougher) the cut. However, there should never be fewer than 3 teeth passing through the wood and usually no more than 12 (except when ripping thick boards or resawing). Here's a handy chart for quick reference.

tpi	Minimum Material Thickness
32	³⁄₃₂ in.
24	⅛ in.
18	⁵⁄₃₂ in.
14	¼ in.
10	⁵⁄₁₆ in.
8	⅜ in.
6	½ in.
4	¾ in.
3	1 in.
2	1½ in.

TOOTH SHAPE

The form of the tooth is the most important factor in how a blade cuts.

Regular		° rake angle
Skip		° rake angle
Hook		Positive rake angle
Variable		Teeth vary in number (tpi) but not in shape

Hook Tooth

Hook-tooth blades have a positive rake angle, resulting in an aggressive cutting action. They typically have few teeth per inch and big gullets that efficiently evacuate the large amounts of sawdust created by the

tooth shape. These are the workhorses of the bandsaw blade family, ideally suited for ripping heavy timbers and resawing wide boards. Hook-tooth blade sizes usually start at a 1/4-in. width. They have fewer teeth per inch than a regular blade and leave a slightly rougher surface.

Variable Pitch

Harmonic vibrations can cause a blade to flutter during a heavy cut, resulting in striated, rough sections of the cut. (See p. 46.) When resawing dense wood or ripping big timbers, the flutter will often come and go without apparent rhyme or reason. *Variable-pitch blades*—a carryover from the metal-cutting industry—are designed to defeat this vibration. The teeth vary in spacing in a repeating pattern, which dampens a blade's tendency to vibrate like a guitar string.

Tooth Set

As a blade cuts through wood, clearance between the blade body and the wood is necessary to help clear away sawdust and to reduce friction between the blade and the wood. The teeth on most saw blades are *set*, or alternately bent sideways, to create a cut that is wider than the blade body. The resulting cut is called the blade *kerf*.

Alternate Set

On a blade with *alternate set*, every other tooth is bent in the same direction, creating a pattern of left-right, left-right. Alternate set is also referred to as *ETS*, or "every tooth set." Regular tooth blades are usually set in this fashion, with a relatively slight set to create a smoother cut. This set works well for crosscutting or sawing tight curves with

---

TOOTH SET

Blade profile	Alternate set	Raker set	Modified raker

Every tooth set (ETS)

pattern: left-right

Every third tooth set

pattern: left-right-straight

Every fifth tooth straight

pattern: left/right/ left-right-straight

narrow blades. Alternate set also works very well for cutting thin stock.

Raker Set

On a *raker set* blade, every third tooth is unset, creating a left-right-straight pattern. The straight tooth rakes the bottom of the kerf, removing the slight ridge left by the set teeth. It also helps clear out sawdust. Raker-set blades cut cleanly and are available in all tooth configurations.

Modified Raker Set

With a *modified raker set*, every fifth tooth is unset, so the pattern is left-right, left-right, straight. The result of the unset fifth tooth is a clean cut with a slightly faster cutting rate than a standard raker set.

Blade Thickness & Width

Blade thickness typically increases with blade width. Bandsaw blades range from a slim 0.014 in. thick up to a very substantial 0.063 in. thick, although most commonly available blades are 0.022 in. to 0.036 in. thick. Narrow, thin blades are best suited for cutting curves in relatively thin material. Thin bandsaw blades, like thin-kerf tablesaw blades, strain the saw less because they are biting into less wood. Therefore, a thin resaw blade may lack a bit of beam strength but will help a low-powered machine saw thick lumber.

Wide, thick blades have the formidable beam strength necessary for heavy sawing tasks like resawing wide boards or heavy timbers. However, the tension required to run these blades puts tremendous strain on a bandsaw frame. Typical 14-in. bandsaws are best able to handle blades up to ³⁄₄ in.

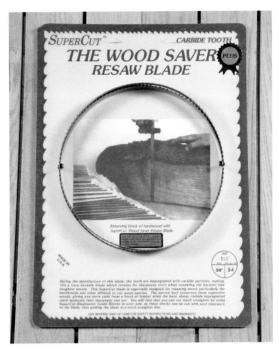

The SuperCut™ Wood Saver blade, with its thin kerf and variable pitch, is designed for resawing.

wide with a maximum thickness of 0.025 in. However, some manufacturers do offer ³⁄₄-in. resaw blades as thick as 0.032 in. for use on a 14-in. saw. Larger saws are designed to handle the higher tensioning demands of thick, wide blades.

Resaw Blades

Resaw blades are designed for the demanding job of ripping thick stock. The best resaw blades have variable tooth spacing (usually 2 to 3 tpi) to help defeat the blade flutter often encountered when resawing wide boards. Aggressive hook-shaped teeth with large gullets help remove the copious sawdust created by resawing.

Resaw blades often have specially treated teeth to ensure long tooth life under the heavy-duty demands of the job. The teeth on spring steel resaw blades are typically heat-hardened for good cutting and decent longevity at a moderate price. Bimetal resaw blades or blades with hard-faced or carbide-impregnated teeth are tougher than spring or carbon steel and will last longer when cutting abrasive woods such as teak or ipe. Blades with attached carbide teeth offer the ultimate durability, but at a steep price. The upside is that most of them can be resharpened, extending their long life further.

Blade Width and Cut Radius

When sawing curves, a blade can sometimes bind in the cut. This comes from trying to cut too tight a radius with too wide a blade. A blade will not bend to form itself around a tight radius. Instead, the trailing rear edge scrapes and burnishes the side of the kerf, creating ridges and impeding smooth cutting action. The friction can create enough heat to scorch the wood and wreck the blade, particularly if it's narrow. To avoid the problem, select an appropriate-width blade for the radius of the cut, as shown in the drawing on the facing page. Rounding the back edges of the blade, as shown on p. 49, can also help.

▶ See *"Stoning a Blade"* on p. 49.

So why not just use a very narrow blade for curved cuts of any radius? Well, you could, but it's hard to follow sweeping curves with a very narrow blade. The extra depth on a wider blade will help you track the cut.

Selecting Blades

Understanding the difference between available bandsaw blades will help you determine the right blade for a specific job. Here's some advice to help you choose a blade of the correct material, tooth shape, pitch, and width.

Blade Material

The choice of blade material depends to some degree on what kind of wood you'll be cutting. A standard high-carbon blade should prove durable enough for general cutting of most North American hardwoods and softwoods, but hard or abrasive woods may require a bimetal blade. For a lot of resawing, a bimetal or carbide blade is a much better choice.

[TIP] **For quick, easy reference, note your saw's blade length on the inside of the wheel house door.**

Width & Thickness

Blade width is entirely determined by the project's need. For cutting lots of curves, a 1/8-in. or 1/4-in. blade works best. For general-purpose use, sawing gentle curves, ripping thin stock, and cutting joinery, you're best served by a 3/8-in. blade. Resawing thick lumber requires great beam strength, so the wider the better. For smaller saws, a 1/2-in. blade will do the job, although it may be slow going in thick stock. When resawing, I typically use a blade at least 3/4 in. wide.

Blade thickness is usually limited to whatever the manufacturer has deemed the proper thickness for any given type and size of blade. For 14-in. saws, it typically ranges from 0.022 in to 0.025 in. For larger saws,

MAXIMUM BLADE WIDTHS FOR CURVE CUTS

To prevent binding and burning, avoid blades that are too wide for the desired curve. Copy this full-scale drawing for quick reference of maximum blade size for the diameters shown.

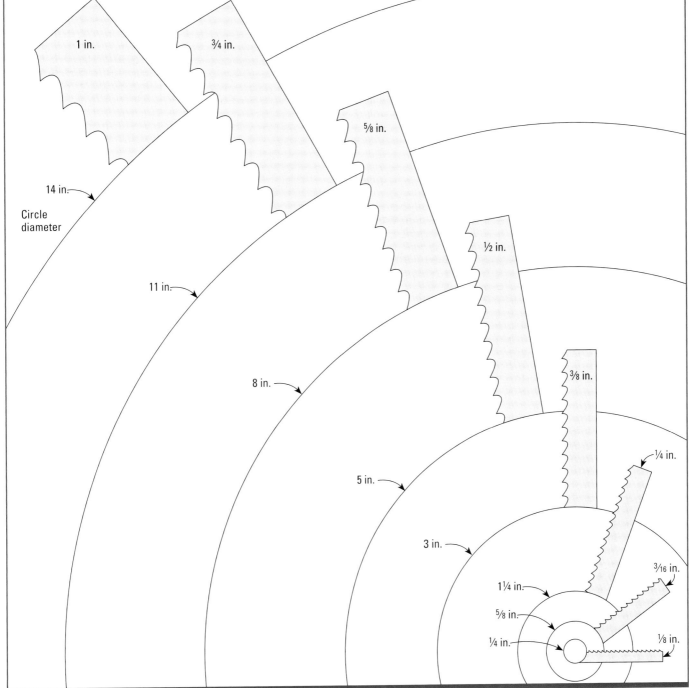

1 in.

¾ in.

⅝ in.

½ in.

⅜ in.

¼ in.

14 in.

Circle
diameter

11 in.

8 in.

5 in.

3 in.

³⁄₁₆ in.

1¼ in.

⅝ in.

¼ in.

⅛ in.

▶ PERFECT PITCH

Here are a few guidelines to help you select a blade with the proper teeth per inch:

- In general, fewer teeth per inch provide a faster but rougher cut. Conversely, more teeth per inch provide a smoother but slower cut.

- Use a higher-pitch (more teeth per inch) blade when sawing extremely dense woods.

- When crosscutting round stock, use a high-pitch blade. The smaller teeth are less likely to aggressively dig into the round stock, spinning it out of control.

- Saw green wood with low-pitch blades; the large gullets are necessary to remove the wet shavings. (Promptly clean the blade when finished to keep it from rusting.)

it's usually 0.032 in. to 0.035 in. When a choice is available, keep in mind that thicker blades provide more beam strength for resawing, while thinner blades provide more curve-cutting agility and consume a bit less horsepower.

Teeth Per Inch

When selecting a blade based on the number of tpi, here's the general rule: The more teeth, the smoother the cut, and the fewer the teeth, the faster the cut. Crosscutting, joinery, and sawing cylindrical stock all benefit from more tpi, while ripping and resawing benefit from fewer tpi. Extremely dense woods cut better with more tpi, while soft, resinous woods are better served by the big gullets on blades with fewer tpi.

Tooth Type

A regular-tooth blade cuts cleanly but slowly due to the 0° rake angle and the small gullets. It's best suited to sawing thin wood and tight curves. A skip-tooth blade with a 0° rake angle cuts faster and nearly as cleanly. It's best suited to gentle curves and combination crosscutting and ripping. A hook-tooth blade cuts fastest but leaves a rougher surface, making it a good choice for general-purpose ripping and resawing.

[TIP] A ¼-in., 4- or 6-tpi hook-tooth blade is my general-purpose blade of choice. One such blade lives on my 14-in. bandsaw most of the time.

Sources

The best sources for good quality bandsaw blades are specialty woodworking tool suppliers or the blade manufacturers themselves. (See Resources on p. 198.) An Internet search or perusal of woodworking magazine advertisers will also yield sources, but beware of shopping for price over quality. Local welding supply shops often carry bulk bandsaw blade material and can make any length blade you need. Although their selection may be limited, a local shop can provide blades for older saws with nonstandard lengths.

Ordering Blades

When ordering blades, I first tally the specifications for my desired blades to expedite the process and ensure that I haven't overlooked anything. Here's an example of the form I use.

Material

Length

Width

Thickness

tpi

Tooth type

Source

Price

A Basic Blade Menu

There's a wide variety of blade sizes and tooth configurations to choose from, as discussed in detail in this chapter. Here are some basic suggestions to get you started.

TYPE OF WORK	BLADE CHOICES	COMMENTS
Tight scrolling	1/8-in. 14 tpi regular tooth	For tightest curves; cuts smoothly but slowly
	1/4-in. 6 tpi regular tooth	For moderate curves; fairly smooth finish
General curved work	1/4-in. 6 tpi hook tooth	Cuts fast, but somewhat roughly
	1/2-in. 6 tpi hook or skip	For gentle, sweeping curves
General ripping	1/2-in. 10 tpi regular tooth	For stock up to 1/2 in. thick; smooth finish
	1/2-in. 4 tpi hook tooth	For stock 3/4 in. to 3 in. thick;
Resawing	1/2-in. to 3/4-in. 2 to 3 tpi (variable)	Variable pitch minimizes blade flutter
	1/2-in. to 3/4-in. 3 tpi hook tooth	Use if a variable-pitch blade isn't available
Joinery	1/2-in. 10 tpi regular tooth	Moderate rip; fairly smooth rip and crosscut finish

Note: Use finer-pitch blades for smooth cuts in dense woods (except for resawing).

Use a brass-bristle brush and blade cleaner to remove gunk from a blade.

Cleaning Blades

Accumulated sawdust and pitch affect a blade's cutting efficiency. Gunk in the gullets impedes extraction of the sawdust, which is then jammed between the blade and the kerf, resulting in power-sapping friction. Built-up detritus on the inner side of the blade can also cause poor blade tracking.

Most tablesaw blade cleaners will work fine for bandsaw blades. Note that some water-based cleaners may create rust if you don't dry the blades completely after cleaning. A light spray coat of a drying nonsilicone-based lubricant such as LPS 1 will keep your blades rust-free during storage.

Storing Blades

Blade storage is often a casual practice, with blades hung together tooth-to-tooth on a nail or piled in a drawer. However, the teeth are relatively delicate and easily damaged, which can cause the blade to behave erratically. The teeth on a folded blade can also suffer damage as they slide against each other in coiled form. To prevent this, wrap a piece of soft wire or blue painter's tape around the coil. (Avoid regular masking tape, which can leave hardened residue over time.)

Store blades in a way that protects the teeth. I use a ceiling-mounted rack that allows hanging blades back-to-back on individual dowels. Alternatively, you can hang separated blades on the wall or store them unstacked on shelves or in drawers.

[TIP] Avoid storing blades in damp conditions. The tiny pits caused by rust will quickly degrade and dull a sharp edge.

A ceiling-mounted storage rack keeps blades neatly organized and safely out of the way.

Breaking Blades

Blade breakage should be rare. In 30 years of working wood, I haven't broken more than a handful of blades. And that was due to inappropriate blade choice or abuse, such as overstressing a blade by forcing it to perform feats for which it was ill suited. Forcing a blade creates heat, which can work-harden the blade, causing cracks and imminent failure.

Here are the golden rules for avoiding blade breakage:

• Use a sharp blade that's suited to the work at hand.
• Set the guides correctly, and don't over-tension the blade.
• Cut using straight-on feed pressure only. Don't apply side pressure and don't force the blade.

• Support your work adequately, keeping it tight to the table at the cut point.
• Secure cylindrical stock to prevent rolling.

Blade Repair

Although a broken blade can be rewelded, there is usually additional damage, such as severe bending or kinking, that makes a repair questionable. It's also generally not cost-effective, since most new blades are reasonably priced. If you damage an expensive blade, such as a carbide-toothed resaw blade, you can ship it back to the manufacturer for repair or have the work done at a local saw shop.

> ⚠ **WARNING If a blade breaks, shut off the power at the switch or plug and listen for the upper wheel to stop spinning before opening the wheel house door.**

Blade Guides

Squaring Guides

Replacing Guides

➤ Squaring Euro-Style Rollers (p. 79)

➤ Squaring Block Guides (p. 80)

➤ Installing Aftermarket Guides (p. 81)

A BANDSAW HAS TWO SETS of blade guides to minimize blade deflection in use. One set of guides is mounted above the table on a guidepost that adjusts in height to accommodate stock of different thickness. The other set is fixed in mounts just below the table. Each set of guides consists of a pair of *side guides* that flank the blade to control side-to-side motion. These guides take the form of either rollers or blocks. A *thrust guide* sits behind the blade to maintain the blade's beam strength and resist its rearward motion.

In this section, I'll discuss the various types of guides and how to adjust and maintain them. We'll also take a look at the selection of aftermarket upgrade and specialty guides to help you get the most from your saw.

A set of bandsaw blade guides consists of a guide on either side of the blade and a support bearing behind the blade.

Two Basic Types

There are basically two types of guides: block and roller. Bandsaws typically come equipped with a roller thrust guide accompanied by either block or roller side guides. Roller guides provide either edge support or face support, depending on their orientation in the guide assembly.

Block guides provide the greatest support area because the blade is almost completely supported by the blocks' surface. European-style roller side guides also provide good support because of their relatively large face contact with the blade (although they are fussier to adjust than block guides). Edge-support roller guides offer support only at the intersecting tangential point between the blade and the roller. However, they compensate for this by allowing direct contact with the blade, theoretically preventing any wayward movement at all.

Block Guides

Block guides are easy to mount and adjust and have traditionally served as side guides for most of the bandsaw's history. They're relatively inexpensive to buy or easy to make if you want to replace or upgrade them. Block guides offer good support and can be easily configured to accommodate narrow blades. Block guides are available in several different materials, including steel, plastic, phenolic, and ceramic. You can also make them yourself from wood.

Steel Guides

Many bandsaws come equipped with steel blocks for side guides. When properly face-dressed and accurately set, steel blocks provide good blade support and long wear

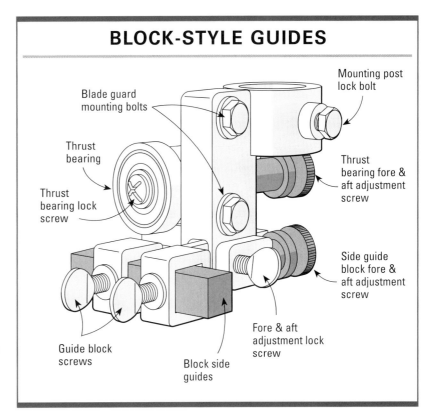

BLOCK-STYLE GUIDES

Mounting post lock bolt

Blade guard mounting bolts

Thrust bearing

Thrust bearing fore & aft adjustment screw

Thrust bearing lock screw

Side guide block fore & aft adjustment screw

Guide block screws

Block side guides

Fore & aft adjustment lock screw

Traditional guide blocks are simple, effective, and easily repaired or upgraded with replacement blocks.

The angled steel guides on this antique Walker-Turner are held in place by individual guide covers.

Test the fit of shop-made hard maple guide blocks before soaking them in oil.

between refacings. It's a common misconception that steel guides create the excessive heat that leads to premature blade failure. However, the truth is that properly adjusted guides with accurately trued faces will not generate undue friction and heat unless the sawyer is performing work beyond the blade's capabilities, resulting in excessive rubbing of the blade against the blocks.

[TIP] Unlike wood, plastic, or phenolic blocks, steel blocks can ruin blade teeth upon errant contact.

Lubricant-Soaked Hardwood

Many early-model bandsaws came equipped with hardwood guide blocks, typically made of beech or hard maple. To minimize friction, they were usually soaked in kerosene, paraffin, or light machine oil. Hardwood blocks provide good blade support with little friction. They're easy to dress and cost practically nothing to replace.

Making wood guide blocks is as simple as choosing a dense hardwood, cutting the blocks to size, and throwing them in a can full of lubricant for a few weeks (I prefer light machine oil). The lubricant will eventually permeate the entire piece of wood, providing a slick surface even after multiple face-dressings. Wood guide blocks are a particularly good replacement for antique steel guides that may no longer be available.

Plastic

Plastic guides are showing up as original equipment on some new bandsaws. Offering good support with minimal friction, plastic guides wear quickly but are easy to reface

Soaking maple guide blocks in a jarful of light machine oil or kerosene for a couple of weeks will make the guides self-lubricating.

and cheap to replace. They will provide decent service during their short life.

Phenolic

Phenolic-impregnated fiber blocks contain a dry lubricant that creates a low-friction blade glide surface. Available only as side guides, they're sold under the name Cool Blocks and are produced by several manufacturers. Adjusted to lightly ride against the blade, phenolic blocks provide great support without creating additional heat. To some extent, they can act as scrapers to help keep a blade from gumming up when cutting resinous wood. Phenolic blocks can be set up to literally trap a very narrow blade that would be difficult to control with roller side guides.

Plastic guides are effective and easy on blades, although the material wears relatively quickly.

Plastic, phenolic-impregnated, and wood guides allow entrapment of narrow blades for better guidance when cutting tight-radius curves.

Laguna Tools offers a complete ceramic guide assembly replacement. (The blade guard is removed here for clarity.)

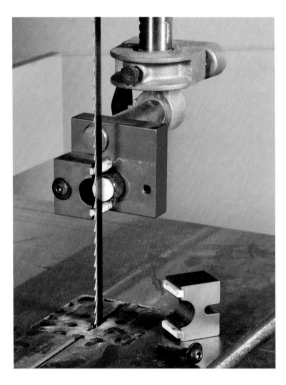

Ceramic

Ceramic guides are low-friction, long-wearing pieces of ceramic material. Because they act as heat sinks, they can ride lightly against the blade for precise, cool-running control. Available as optional equipment on some new saws, they are also offered as replacements for traditional block guides or roller thrust guides. You can also get a complete unique ceramic guide assembly to replace your factory guide systems.

Ceramic is the only material that allows a block to be used as a thrust guide in place of a roller bearing. The thrust block can be set tight to the back edge of the blade, making setup simple and reducing the chance of blade twist due to non-coplanar thrust guides.

Because they can be set so closely to the blade, ceramic guides can act as blade scrapers to clean gummy residue off the blade when cutting resinous woods.

Roller Guides

Roller guides are typically ball-bearing guides that use the face or edge of the bearing assembly to support the blade. Roller guides allow direct contact between the blade and the guide without creating heat or incurring frictional drag. However, most guide manufacturers recommend a few thousandths of an inch clearance between blade and guide. Some bearings are true sealed ball bearings, which prevent fine-dust infiltration that can impede bearing rotation. Others are simply ball bearings with a dust shield or cover.

ROLLER BEARING GUIDES

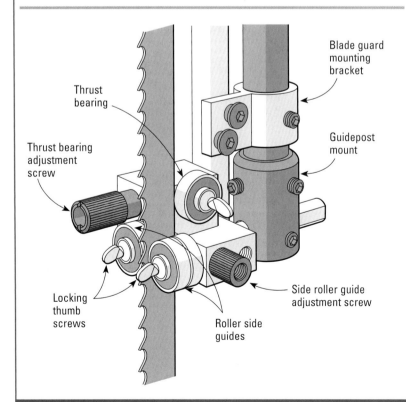

Thrust bearing

Thrust bearing adjustment screw

Locking thumb screws

Roller side guides

Blade guard mounting bracket

Guidepost mount

Side roller guide adjustment screw

Edge-Bearing Rollers

With edge-bearing rollers, the perimeter of the bearing serves as the support surface. When used as side guides, edge-bearing rollers offer good support across the width of all but the narrowest blades. Blade and bearing meet at a tangential point with negligible frictional losses.

The benefits of edge-bearing rollers are twofold. First, the bearing is used as it is designed: to provide support at its perimeter. Second, the bearings can be adjusted for zero-clearance contact with the blade, resulting in very precise setups. The downside of a zero-clearance setup is reduced bearing life due to constant rotation, even when the blade is freewheeling. Nonetheless, I consider this a fair tradeoff for quick setup and increased accuracy.

When used as thrust guides, edge-bearing rollers allow the same easy, zero-clearance setup, allowing the blade to continually run against the guide. This provides good thrust support and accurate coplanar adjustment of guides for excellent control during resawing or heavy ripping of thick planks.

Face-Bearing Rollers

Face-bearing rollers have long been used as thrust guides on bandsaws. With these rollers, the blade rides across the face of the bearing instead of on the perimeter. Face-bearing rollers offer a larger area of support than edge-bearing rollers, but they rely on well-lubricated bearings and an accurate setup to work well. Bearings that freeze up or that won't turn freely often end up scarred from the blade, with the resulting grooves causing rough blade operation and poor support.

The large thrust bearing on the Carter Precision 20 blade guide is actually a large wheel pressed onto a sealed roller bearing, providing generous thrust support.

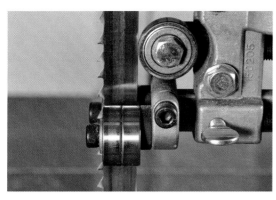

Side roller bearings on this Powermatic® saw offer good support for a wide blade, and the edge-bearing thrust guide directly contacts the blade for constant thrust support.

A face-bearing thrust guide that doesn't turn freely upon blade contact can end up scarred, grooved, and useless.

EUROPEAN-STYLE ROLLER GUIDES

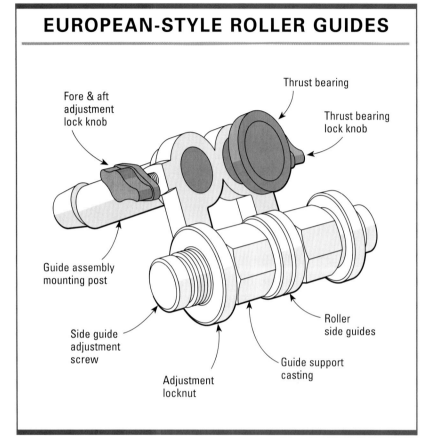

Fore & aft adjustment lock knob

Thrust bearing

Thrust bearing lock knob

Guide assembly mounting post

Side guide adjustment screw

Adjustment locknut

Guide support casting

Roller side guides

European-Style Guides

European-style roller side guides and roller thrust guides are simply wheels fixed to axles that rotate in their bushings. In operation, they are similar to ball bearings in that the support surface revolves during contact with the blade. This reduces friction and heat and offers good support when set up properly. Unfortunately, side-guide mounts are not always accurately machined, resulting in wheels that are not parallel to each other and that offer little support. This can make them hard to adjust and can actually cause the blade to track poorly.

The thrust wheels offer good support but require frequent attention to ensure that they spin freely. Occasionally clean away the sawdust that accumulates between the wheel and the bushing housing. Remove each axle, blow out the bushings, and then apply a drop or two of router-bearing oil. The thrust

▶ EUROPEAN-STYLE ROLLER GUIDES

European-style roller guides became very popular in the 1990s, when welded-steel bandsaws from Italy and Central Europe started making their way to the United States. Correctly machined and set up, these guides provide good side and rear blade support. However, their reputation took a beating when poorly engineered versions started showing up on low-price bandsaws. These inferior guides were difficult to adjust,

and their thrust bearings often froze up in response to the slightest sawdust buildup between the rear of the roller and the bushing housing.

Today Euro-style guides have practically disappeared in favor of ceramic block or roller bearing guides. Currently, only a few manufacturers (Mini-Max, Felder®, Agazzani, and General®) still produce them for the American market. Fortunately, they are high-quality versions.

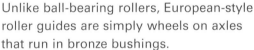

Unlike ball-bearing rollers, European-style roller guides are simply wheels on axles that run in bronze bushings.

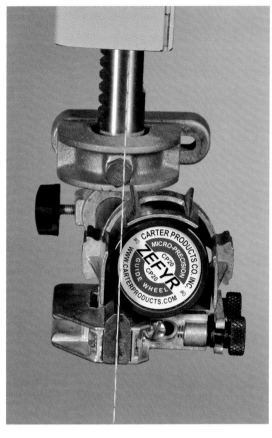

Ideally, a blade should run close to the edge of a thrust bearing to encourage the bearing's rotation under feed load.

wheels can also be refaced if necessary, as long as the groove damage isn't too deep.

Thrust Bearings

Thrust guides are typically face-bearing rollers, mounted perpendicular to the blade, although some saws utilize edge-bearing rollers. Thrust guides endure high loads when resawing or ripping heavy stock because they're providing substantial support to maintain the blade's beam strength.

Supporting a blade with the face of a bearing instead of its edge is a less-than-ideal solution. In theory, the bearing rotates in response to the blade sliding across the edge of its face, resulting in minimum friction between the blade and bearing.

However, in practice, the bearing must be kept in top working order to prevent dust and grime from slowing or stopping its rotation and allowing the blade to wear grooves in the bearing face. This can cause tracking problems as the blade bounces around in the intermittently rotating grooves.

Edge-bearing thrust guides are less problematic but still require attention to ensure that they rotate freely. If a bearing freezes up, the back of a blade can create a groove in the rim. The tiny area of blade-to-bearing contact can also cause mushrooming of the blade's rear edge under heavy load conditions such as heavy ripping. Using a hard-back blade virtually eliminates this problem.

Aftermarket Replacement Guides

As important as they are, some original equipment guides aren't up to the task of accurately guiding and controlling the blade. Fortunately, a variety of aftermarket guides are available from various manufacturers. They range from simple replacement blocks for standard guide systems to complete guide assemblies that replace the original components. Here is just a sampling of what the market offers.

Block Guides

Heavy-duty guide assemblies like Carter's Micro-Precision Model 20 replace the entire guide assembly. The oversized thrust bearing provides great support for the blade, and the self-lubricating metal rub-block side guides will resist wear under heavy loading situations. Carter offers a wide spectrum of guide configurations for virtually any size saw.

Roller Guides

Aftermarket roller guide assemblies offer a quick and relatively inexpensive replacement for original equipment block guides. Carter

Industrial-strength block guide kits like Carter's Micro-Precision Model 20 replace the entire stock guide assembly.

Aftermarket roller guide kits contain all of the brackets and mounts for easy, precise replacement of guide block assemblies.

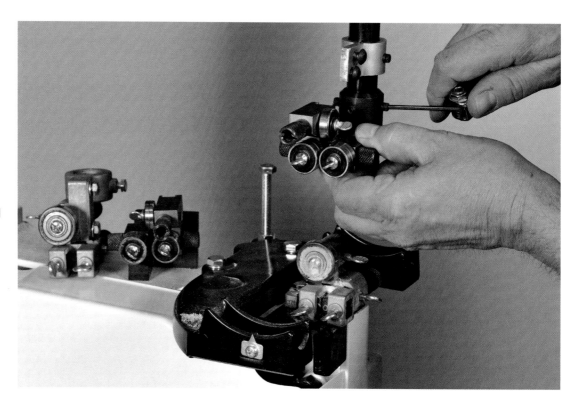

Products sells a variety of replacement assemblies, including their AccuRight™ upgrade kit designed specifically for 14-in. bandsaws.

Ceramic Guides

Ceramic guides are available to replace original equipment guide blocks or as complete replacement assemblies. While Laguna Tools offers a complete replacement package for popular bandsaws, Spaceage Ceramic Guideblocks® are available as replacement block guides for most popular bandsaws.

Phenolic & Plastic Blocks

Phenolic and plastic guide blocks offer a low-cost, effective guide block upgrade. Simply remove the factory guides and insert the new blocks. They're easy to true up,

they won't harm the blade upon accidental contact, and their self-lubricating qualities allow direct contact with the blade. Olson® and SuperCut are two companies offering replacement blocks to fit most popular bandsaws.

[TIP] Because of their scraping action in use, block guides are ideally suited for working with resinous woods, which would gum up roller guides.

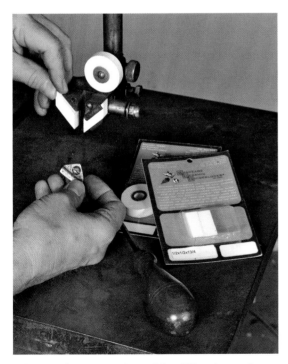

Aftermarket ceramic guides (like these from Spaceage Ceramic) are available for most bandsaws, old or new.

Olson Cool Blocks® are self-lubricating and phenolic-impregnated and are available for many popular bandsaws.

SuperCut plastic replacement blocks, made from nylon, are designed to outlast stock plastic blocks.

Iturra Bandrollers are roller side guide roller replacements for typical ½-in. x ½-in. block guides. They're simple to install in the original guide block holders.

The single, grooved roller of the Carter Stabilizer guides blades narrower than ¼ in. to perform tight curve-cutting.

Specialty Rollers

A couple of interesting aftermarket guide options are available for 14-in. bandsaws with square block guides. Iturra Bandrollers are small-diameter sealed ball bearings mounted in a ½-in.-square aluminum holder that fits most 14-in. cast-iron bandsaws. Simple to install and relatively inexpensive, they mount in the original guide block holders. Bandrollers aren't recommended for use with blades narrower than ¼ in., but they offer good support for resawing with blades ½ in. or wider. Due to their small-diameter bearings and close proximity to the bearing holder, sawdust needs to be cleared away frequently to prevent clogging the bearings.

Another handy replacement guide is the Carter Stabilizer®, which is designed for use with blades ¼ in. or narrower. The Stabilizer replaces the one-piece upper side-guide holder on typical 14-in. bandsaws. The single grooved roller sits behind the blade, providing both thrust support and side support. (The lower bandsaw guides aren't used.) The roller's shallow groove provides adequate side support while allowing the blade flexibility for tight scroll cutting.

Squaring Euro-Style Rollers

As shown in the drawing on p. 74, a European-style roller guide assembly consists of a double-armed guide support casting that carries the thrust bearing and both roller side guide holders.

European-style roller guides offer good blade support when they are correctly adjusted. The side wheels need to be nearly dead parallel top-to-bottom **(A)** while angling slightly inward at the front **(B)**. If the guides are out of parallel top-to-bottom **(C)**, loosen the screws that secure the roller side guide holders to the support casting **(D)**, and set the guides parallel to a tensioned bandsaw blade. There is usually enough free-play between the mounting surfaces to make the proper correction.

If the guides angle inward at the rear, blade support behind the gullets is compromised. To correct the problem, first remove one roller guide holder, noting that it mounts on two narrow rails on the support casting **(E)**. Blacken the rails with a marker for reference **(F)**, and then carefully file them until the correct wheel positioning is achieved **(G)**. Check your progress frequently, as removing a tiny amount of material can make a big difference in the holder's position. Make sure to remove the same amount of material from each rail to avoid creating a twisted mounting surface.

A

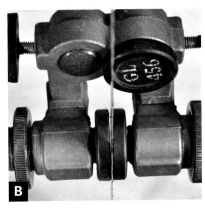

B

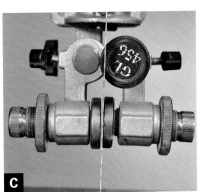

C

D

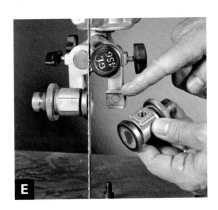

E

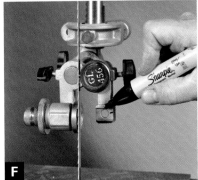

F

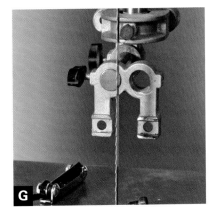

G

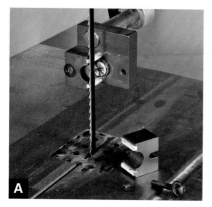

A

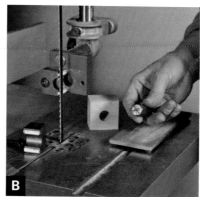

B

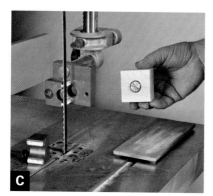

C

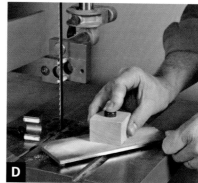

D

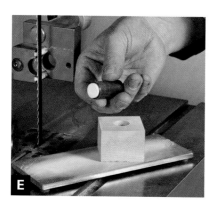

E

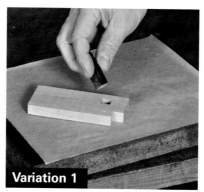

Variation 1

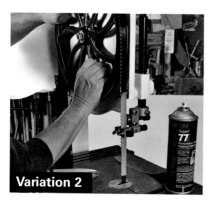

Variation 2

Squaring Block Guides

Block guides offer great blade support when they have smooth faces that are properly squared to the block body. Whether metal, wood, ceramic, phenolic, or plastic, all guide blocks suffer wear from frequent contact with the blade, which creates grooves and nonparallel block faces.

The face of this ceramic thrust guide has slight grooves that need to be removed to provide consistent blade support **(A)**. (The guide has been rotated over time to present a smooth section to the back of the blade.) To dress the face flat, make a simple holder by boring a hole the same diameter as the guide block through a piece of maple **(B)**. Use a drill press to ensure the hole is parallel to the face of the block, and then insert the guide into the hole **(C)**. Rub the assembly over a diamond plate **(D)** to remove the grooves and flatten the bearing face **(E)**.

You can dress metal, wood, phenolic, or plastic side guides in the same fashion, using 150-grit sandpaper instead of a diamond plate.

[VARIATION 1] To dress square guide blocks, I use a shopmade hardwood holder with a ½-in.-sq. through-mortise and a ½-in.-sq. notch cut in one corner to provide two ways to hold a guide block.

[VARIATION 2] Sometimes a saw's guide block assembly doesn't hold side guide faces parallel to each other. In that case, you can true the block faces parallel to the blade. Use spray adhesive to glue a piece of 150-grit sandpaper to both sides of a blade that's wider than the blocks. Lightly pinch the blocks together against the sandpaper at the same time, and work the blade back and forth like a file to true the faces parallel.

Installing Aftermarket Guides

Replacing stock equipment block guides with aftermarket guides is a relatively easy project. The kits typically include all the brackets, guards, and hardware needed to make the change **(A)**.

Start by removing the bandsaw blade, table, and any guards that may interfere with installation. Remove the original guides and their mounting brackets **(B)**. Slide the new blade guard bracket high up on the upper guide post for the moment, and lightly tighten the set screw **(C)**. Mount the upper guide assembly holder on the guidepost and lightly tighten its set screws **(D)**. Lower the blade guard bracket into position directly above the guide mount and securely tighten it.

Install the lower guide assembly mount and snug it up without tightening the screws **(E)**. (The bracket may have to be shifted during final setup.) Install the upper and lower guide assemblies **(F)**, adjust the side guides to their widest opening position, and move the thrust bearing as far back as possible.

Install and tension a ½-in. or wider blade. Use the blade as a centerline to adjust the guide holders. Move the side guides close to the blade and tighten them enough to eliminate any play **(G)**. Check for parallelism with the blade and, if necessary, tap the lower guide mount side-to-side to center the side guides. Make any adjustments and tighten the guide mount, being careful not to shift it out of position **(H)**. Next, move to the upper guide mount, centering and securing it with its three set screws **(I)**.

Finally, set the thrust bearings, install the blade guards, mount the table, and perform the standard guide setup procedure as explained in Section 2.

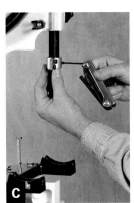

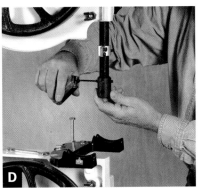

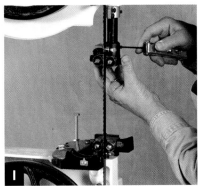

Safety

THE BANDSAW IS A RELATIVELY SAFE power tool, but it is not benign. On the one hand, it can't kick back workpieces like a tablesaw and there are no spinning shafts, blades, or bits that can become entangled with digits or limbs. However, it does have a moving blade with lots of sharp teeth. Never forget that the bandsaw is a butcher's favorite meat-cutting tool because it quickly and effortlessly cuts through flesh and bone.

In this section, I'll discuss techniques and accessories for keeping you safe at the bandsaw. Understanding the bandsaw is critical because the best protection is an operator who is familiar with the tool, its operation, and its potential dangers.

Know Thy Saw

The old adage "When all else fails, read the instructions" should never apply to a tool that can maim. Read your saw's owner's manual. Most contain setup advice and operational cautions that serve as the first line of defense against catastrophic mistakes that can result from simple oversights. Unfortunately, some owner's manuals are pretty sketchy. After gleaning all you can from one, it's wise to spend some time reading pertinent magazine articles, books like this one, and articles found through reliable woodworking Web sites like *Fine Woodworking* (www.finewoodworking.com).

Read your owner's manual. It provides the first line of defense against accidents.

Bandsaw articles in magazines and books can offer lots of safety advice and techniques for better bandsaw setups and performance.

[TIP] Copies of bandsaw manuals are often available from the manufacturer or from websites such as Old Wood-Working Machines (www.owwm.com) and eBay (www.ebay.com).

Make sure you can find the power switch quickly, without fumbling.

Familiarizing yourself with the intricacies of a bandsaw will not only keep you safe, but it will also make you a better craftsman. Knowing your saw's strengths is important, but so is knowing its limitations.

Safety includes things like avoiding cutting material that is beyond the saw's horsepower or size capacity. For example, plopping a 100-lb. log on a 14-in. bandsaw table isn't usually a good idea. Forcing a saw to perform beyond its capabilities often results in ruined work, broken machinery, or personal injury.

Keep in mind that the most important safety feature on a bandsaw is the power switch. Finding it easily should become second nature to you. You don't want to have to grope around for it in an emergency.

SAFETY BASICS

- Unplug the saw to do any work on it.

- Let saw wheels stop completely before opening doors or adjusting guides.

- Never operate the saw when tired, intoxicated, or under the influence of drugs.

- Focus on the job. Avoid interruptions.

- Take your time. Hurrying can cause harm and mistakes.

- Stay alert. Use an anti-fatigue mat, take breaks, stay hydrated, and know when to quit.

The Bandsaw Workstation

The location of your bandsaw and the way you set up the work area is just as important as the setup of the saw itself. Accessories such as auxiliary feed supports and a mobile base can make for safer, more convenient work. Good lighting also contributes to safety and accuracy.

Saw Placement

A bandsaw's small footprint allows you to tuck it into a corner or other small space, but this can lead to encumbrances when sawing large or long stock. There are few maneuvers more aggravating and potentially dangerous than your board hitting a wall or other obstacle when you're a few inches from finishing a cut. At best, you'll have to shut off the saw, reposition the machine, and then finish the cut. In a worse case, the collision can ruin the cut and possibly bind or break the blade. One good solution is to use a mobile base, which allows you to easily relocate the saw for necessary cutting clearance. Remember to lock the wheels before cutting.

Work Area Setup

Avoid clutter around your work area, and don't use the saw as a leaning post for lumber. As you work, clean offcut pieces from the floor, especially the small odd-shaped remnants of scroll cutting. Tripping over detritus can result in ruined work or injury.

When cutting long stock, always use an outfeed support. An unsupported board can lever upward enough to hinder safe, accurate feeding. The leveraged upward pressure against the guides can also damage them or at least knock them out of alignment. For convenience, keep tools for blade changes and guide adjustment mounted on the saw with magnets. Use an anti-fatigue mat to reduce stress and help maintain your focus during long stints at the saw.

[TIP] Roller stands work well for supporting straight cuts but are troublesome for curved cuts. Unidirectional roller ball supports will work for both.

Allow adequate room around your saw for the particular cut you're making.

Always provide support for long stock, particularly on the outfeed side.

Lighting

Proper lighting is important for both safety and cutting accuracy. Poor lighting creates eyestrain and makes it harder to follow cut lines, particularly on curved work. Ideally a bandsaw should be placed directly under a bright light source that illuminates the blade area with no shadows, even when you are standing next to the saw. A saw-mounted task light is ideal, especially if it has a flexible arm for accurate positioning.

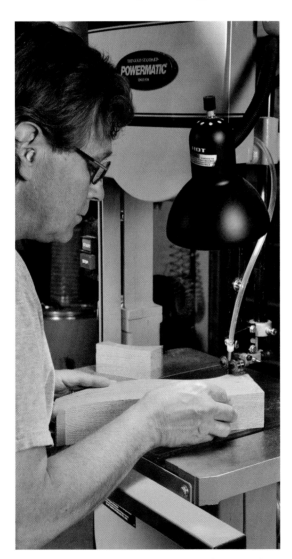

A saw-mounted worklamp provides good task-lighting for guide setup and sawing.

Safety Gear

We might spend a lot of time maintaining our woodworking tools and equipment but fail to take care of the most important shop asset: ourselves. Make sure to outfit yourself with eye, ear, and lung protection to protect your physical well-being and increase your comfort at the saw.

Eye & Ear Protection

Without exception, always wear eye protection when working with power tools. Why risk a stray splinter blinding an eye when wearing glasses can eliminate the risk? Although a bandsaw doesn't hurl sawdust at the operator the way a tablesaw does, it still creates enough ambient dust to cause serious eye irritation.

A bandsaw isn't typically as noisy as a tablesaw or router, but it can still produce decibel levels high enough to damage your hearing. And running dust collection compounds the noise. I keep several pairs of earmuffs placed around my shop so that I'm never more than an arm's reach from good hearing protection.

> ⚠ **WARNING Don't ignore the risk of hearing damage, accumulative and irreversible.**

Keep earmuffs or other hearing protection close at hand so you'll use it.

3M's model N95 8210 disposable paper respirator works well for containing fine wood dust.

Dust Mask

Bandsaws can create choking clouds of fine dust that will infiltrate every corner of the shop, every crease in your clothes, and every bronchiole in your lungs. Ripping and resawing produce particularly large volumes of dust. Wear a dust mask if your dust collection system isn't up to containing the dust the saw is creating. Inexpensive nuisance dust masks are seldom adequate. Instead, use a mask that is designed for controlling wood dust. To prevent steaming up your safety glasses, look for a mask with double straps and a bendable nose bridge. I use a 3M N95 8210 Plus particulate respirator. It's a reasonably priced disposable paper mask that works well and is readily available through most supply houses.

[TIP] Learn how to use a neti pot and saline solution to clean accumulated sawdust from your nasal and sinus cavities at day's end. (Search "neti pot" on the Internet.)

Dress for Success

A bandsaw may not have a spinning blade or whirling cutters, but the fast-moving blade can still snag loose clothing or dangling jewelry. Drawstrings on hooded sweatshirts are another easily snagged danger, and loose shirtsleeves can quickly become entangled in the blade's teeth. For the same reason, reading glasses, safety glasses, or earplugs should never be dangled from the neck on a retainer strap.

Never, ever wear gloves when pushing lumber past blades or cutters. Gloves can be easily snagged by a cutter, and they add unaccustomed size to our hands, reducing those instinctive safe-space margins. They also prevent the important tactile feedback we receive through our hands during the cutting operation. Gloves are fine for moving lumber around the shop, but when the motor starts, take off the gloves.

Dust Collection

Connecting your bandsaw to a good shop vacuum or central dust collector will go a long way toward containing nose-clogging dust and keeping the workspace clean. Bandsaws produce very fine sawdust that, when scattered around a smooth shop floor, can become slippery. Losing one's footing while sawing is a dangerous thing.

Newer bandsaws typically have good dust collection hookup points. However, an older saw may require fabricating your own dust collection apparatus. A vacuum hose simply rigged close to the bottom guides will do a reasonably good job. Mounting a 4-in.-dia. dust collector hose on a portable stand positioned behind and close to the lower guides will also work.

An old camera tripod, a block of wood, and a zip tie can be used to rig a shop-vacuum hose close to the bottom guides.

Safety Accessories

Push sticks, table sleds, feather boards, hold-downs, outfeed supports, and other accessories are primarily designed to keep your hands out of harm's way, but they also improve technique, which results in better work. The right accessories partnered with common sense provide the best defenses against bandsaw accidents.

Push Sticks

Any power tool with a moving blade or other cutter demands the use of a push stick when your fingers approach the danger zone.

> ### ▶ BLADE CHANGE SAFETY
>
> **For compact storage,** blades are typically coiled, or "folded," into a tight loop of steel edged with hundreds of very sharp teeth. Because of this, blade changes begin and end with the potentially dangerous maneuver or folding and unfolding the blade, as shown on p. 52. To avoid injury, remember the following:
>
> - Always wear gloves when handling blades.
>
> - Uncoil a blade in an area clear of obstructions and other people.
>
> - Don't clench a blade. Hold it only tightly enough to maneuver it into its coiled or uncoiled form.
>
> - Always secure a coiled blade with a twist tie or tape.
>
> - Store blades safely away from shop traffic.

Try to avoid pushing stock past the blade using your bare hands; it's just too easy to slip, and results can be devastating. Consider push sticks disposable, cutting into them when necessary to follow through on the cut when working with thin or narrow stock. (See Section 6 for more push stick methods and tips.) Push sticks are also helpful for keeping stock tight to the rip fence.

Use a push stick when working close to the blade. It works well for keeping stock tight against the fence when ripping long, narrow stock.

Use a miter gauge for safe, accurate crosscuts. An auxiliary fence that reaches to the blade aids in sawing small or short stock.

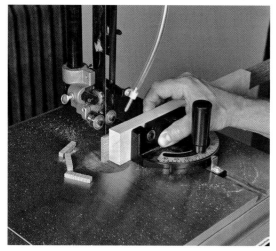

Multiple small parts can be accurately sawn and safely handled using a table sled. After completing a cut, the blade is fully guarded by this sled's fence.

Miter Gauge

A miter gauge provides a safe way of making accurate straight or angled crosscuts without endangering your hands. The gauge provides a backrest to support the stock as it's pushed past the blade. In addition to accuracy, the sturdy support eliminates blade binding caused by inadvertent mishandling of unsupported stock. Miter gauges work well for holding small or short stock, especially when equipped with a sacrificial fence that provides support close to the blade.

Small Parts Sled

Like a miter gauge, a table sled offers good stock support for crosscutting. But a sled has the advantage of providing support on both sides of the blade. This eliminates the possibility of pinching and safely carries the offcut away from the blade. At the end of the cut, the blade is buried in the fence, allowing safe removal of offcuts.

Zero-Clearance Insert

Zero-clearance table inserts prevent small offcuts from tumbling into the lower guides or jamming between the blade and wheel. Just as important, a zero-clearance insert provides stock support right up to the blade, which makes for safer scroll-cutting of small pieces and better compound-cutting.

Featherboard for Resawing

Safe, accurate resawing demands vertical control of the board. A featherboard can keep stock securely positioned against the fence, allowing you to concentrate on proper feed speed without worrying about the stock tipping.

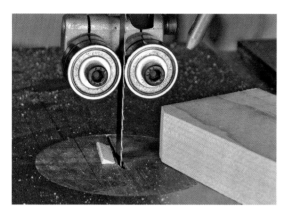

A zero-clearance table insert provides work-piece support right up to the blade and prevents small offcuts from jamming in the lower guides.

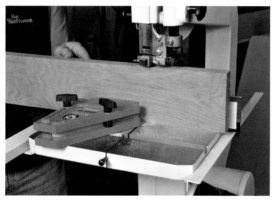

Featherboards will keep tall stock tight to the fence, ensuring safe and accurate work.

V-Block for Round Stock

The first time I crosscut a dowel on a bandsaw, I was shocked when the blade grabbed the dowel and spun it out of my grip, twisting and jamming the blade in the cut and destroying both it and the dowel. A V-block provides secure support, resulting in safe, accurate crosscuts of round stock.

Pre-Flight Checklist

Before a session with any of my bandsaws, I perform a quick check of the saw systems to

> ## WHEN A BLADE BREAKS
>
> **If a blade breaks** when the saw is running, it usually exits to the right of the saw. For safety's sake, avoid standing there any time you're using the saw. If a blade does break, hit the power switch immediately. If it seems dangerous to be near the saw, move away and unplug it instead. Stay away from the saw until the wheels come to a full stop. Keep in mind that a free-wheeling upper wheel can coast inaudibly for quite a while in a noisy shop, so to be safe, wait for a few minutes.

Use the proper jig to keep round work-pieces under control. Here, a V-block provides a safe platform for crosscutting dowels.

make sure everything is ready to go. A saw that's started up with an inappropriate blade, inadequate blade tension, or guides that are loose or incorrectly set is an invitation to a show you don't want to see. (You might want to copy the "Safety Checklist" on p. 90 and tape it to your saw.)

Before turning on your saw, make sure you can answer "yes" to the following:

1. Blade tensioned and tracking properly?

2. Appropriate blade and tooth direction?

3. Blade guides adjusted and secure?

4. Wheel house doors latched and blade guards in place?

5. Push stick at hand?

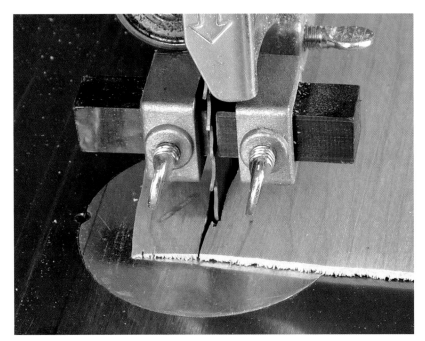

A poor combination of blade and workpiece can result in danger, such as a large blade that may suddenly split thin wood, sending your hand toward the blade.

Use an Appropriate, Sharp Blade

Installing the proper blade for the project at hand makes for a better job and safer cutting. Mistakes in this department can be costly. For example, feeding thin stock into a resaw blade with big teeth can cause a ragged, splintery cut and erratic feeding. The wood may even split, creating a sudden change in feed rate that can cause your hand to skid toward the blade. Conversely, resawing with a narrow, fine-tooth blade may cause you to exert more feed pressure than the blade can handle, resulting in blade twist and a bowed cut that exits the side of a board near an unwary hand.

Use only sharp blades. When using a dull, slow-cutting blade, the tendency is to compensate by using excessive feed force. This leads to wandering cuts and can even knock guides out of whack or cause narrow blades to break. Also, a sudden release of feed pressure at the end of the cut can put your hands at risk.

Blade Direction & Tension

It may sound silly, but before you turn on the bandsaw, make sure the teeth are pointing toward the table. A backward (inside-out) blade can go unnoticed until a slow, smoking cut brings it to your attention.

Before starting the saw, also make sure the blade is tensioned. Many new bandsaws have de-tensioning devices to relax the blade when the saw isn't being used. It's easy to forget a blade is de-tensioned, and the results can be disastrous. A blade can spin off the wheels, damaging your saw and injuring you.

Always check blade tension before starting the saw.

Keep Your Guard Up

The blade guards on a bandsaw are seldom intrusive and offer protection from inadvertent contact with the blade. There's no reason not to keep them in place. This includes the wheel house doors, which should be closed when the saw is running or simply plugged in. A blade can track off the upper wheel faster than you can physically react, and the result can be messy.

The blade guard above the upper guides is extremely important for preventing hand injury. Always follow the cardinal "¼ in. rule." That is, keep the upper guides within ¼ in. of the workpiece. This minimizes blade exposure and affords the best blade control at the same time.

A Safe Stance

Safety starts when you walk up to the bandsaw. Knowing where and how to stand will keep you out of harm's way and maximize

Keep blade guides within ¼ in. above the stock for best safety and cutting performance.

your physical working leverage and your endurance.

Body

I have a motto: "When the mind is weak, the body suffers." So whenever I find my back aching, instead of grumbling about the difficulties of the project, I ask myself, "What was I thinking?" I find that lack of focus often leads to overreaching and over-

Overreaching or overlifting like this can cause back strain. Use feed supports or get other help when handling heavy boards.

For safety, try to adhere to the "4-in. rule" of keeping your hands at least 4 in. away from the blade while sawing. A side benefit is that a wider grip offers better scrolling control.

lifting, which strain the lower back muscles and disks. Pay attention to the way you handle stock. If a board is too heavy, use support rollers or find someone to lend a helping hand.

WARNING Avoid standing to the right side of the table. If a blade breaks, it can exit in this direction much more quickly than you can react.

Hands

Try to keep your hands at least 4 in. away from the blade at all times. Sometimes when scroll-cutting small pieces, you'll have to get closer than that, but following the 4-in. rule is a great general safety practice.

Never place your hands in line with the blade or hook your thumbs on the end of the board when nearing the end of a cut. If the wood suddenly yields to a split or soft spot, your hand could skid into the blade. Use a push stick to finish the cut or pull the workpiece through from the back of the saw.

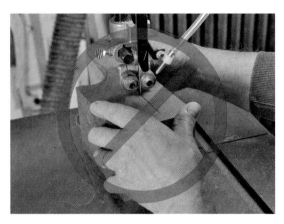

No! Never place your hands in line with the blade like this, especially near the end of a cut. A split or soft spot in the wood could quickly release your hand into the blade.

To finish a cut, either use a push stick or pull the work through from the rear side of the blade.

Never use your hands to support the wood alongside the blade when resawing or ripping. If the blade wanders or blows out the side of the board, as shown in the bottom photo on p. 47, you might not have as much hand as when you started the cut. And don't ever cross your hands when feeding. Always keep your left hand to the left of the blade and your right hand to the right. For better leverage and cutting control, spread your hands as far apart as comfortably possible when cutting heavy or long stock.

Scrollwork often scatters lots of small cutoffs on the table. Never "clear the deck" with your hands when the saw is running. First shut it off and wait for it to coast to a complete stop. And don't think that using a stick or bench brush is okay when the saw is running. Either of these can get caught in the blade, bending or breaking it and possibly ruining your brush.

Safe Stock Feeding

Bandsaw safety can be significantly enhanced with a bit of preplanning. For

For better leverage and cutting control, spread your hands as far apart as comfortably possible.

example, backing a running blade out of a long cut can derail the blade, possibly harming it or your hands. However, a little forethought can prevent this and other problems.

Backing Out of a Cut

My high school woodshop teacher advised us never to back a running bandsaw blade out of a cut. Never. Well, he was both right and wrong. Pulling the work free of a running blade on short cuts such as dovetails or short tenons may be fine; you just have to

Relief cuts produce small waste pieces, allowing blade maneuverability and reducing binding when making tight curves.

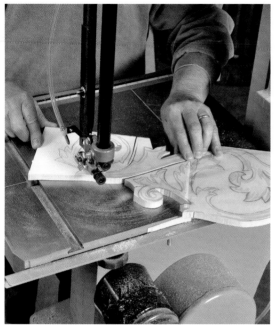

When sawing curves on large pieces, plan your cut approach to avoid the kind of saw frame collision shown here.

do it carefully. Retract the workpiece slowly and evenly to avoid tugging on the blade. If the piece is not pulled straight back from the cut, the blade can bind and pull free of its guides and possibly run off of the wheels.

Scrollwork often involves making a series of intersecting "stop cuts" to remove the waste. On long or curved stop cuts, always turn off the power and wait for the blade to stop before backing out of the cut. It's surprisingly easy to pull the blade off the wheels when they are turning, even slowly. Once the blade has stopped, you can restrain it between the upper guides with a small stick while slowly steering the workpiece free. If the wood has pinched the blade, force a small wedge into the kerf near the entry point to hold it open as you retract the workpiece.

Plan Your Cut Sequence

To avoid binding on tight curves, first make a series of strategically placed relief cuts that will free the waste in small pieces as you work. This allows the blade to proceed unobstructed around the curve. These initial relief cuts should be straight, short, and easy to back out of. This eliminates binding and the need to back the blade out of a long cut.

When making intersecting cuts, saw the short cut first so the waste will be freed at the end of the subsequent long cut. Approach long, curved cuts in a way that allows sufficient swing room. If the work suddenly encounters the saw frame, the blade may go off the line and even pinch or twist.

Sawing Straight

Pushers

Basic Cuts

Dealing with Blade Drift

Using Fences

Tapering

Two Essential Jigs

➤ Making a "Fish" Push Stick (p. 112)

➤ Making a Push Block (p. 113)

➤ Freehand Ripping (p. 115)

➤ Cutting a 3-Sided Notch (p. 116)

➤ Blade Tracking for Drift Adjustment (p. 117)

➤ Adjusting a Fence for Drift (p. 118)

➤ Making a Hi-Lo Fence (p. 119)

➤ Making a Single-Point Fence (p. 120)

➤ Setting Up a Single-Point Fence (p. 122)

➤ A Basic Taper Jig (p. 123)

➤ Using the Basic Taper Jig (p. 123)

➤ Adjustable Taper Jig (p. 124)

➤ Using the Adjustable Taper Jig (p. 126)

➤ A Crosscut Sled (p. 127)

➤ Cradle Jig for Cylindrical Stock (p. 128)

WHILE BANDSAWS ARE RENOWNED for their curve-cutting abilities, they are equally adept at making straight cuts. In fact, their talents for straight cutting rival those of the tablesaw. For example, on a bandsaw you can rip a board freehand to a gauged line—an absolute no-no on a tablesaw. The bandsaw also allows you to make stop cuts that terminate at a 90° angle —something that the geometry of a circular saw blade won't allow. And when it comes to safety, the bandsaw wins hands down, especially for ripping. The downward blade thrust eliminates any danger of kickback, even when ripping slightly twisted boards, which really want to kick back on a tablesaw.

A bandsaw can also perform all manner of straight crosscuts. It's a common misconception that it can't crosscut as cleanly as a tablesaw outfitted with a good combination blade. In fact, with the proper blade, carefully adjusted guides, and a thoughtful cutting procedure, the bandsaw can produce crosscuts that rival those produced by a tablesaw.

Straight cuts on the bandsaw can be made freehand or with fences and jigs. Freehand cutting offers the freedom of following a scribed line by eye, while the use of a fence or jig provides for repeatable cuts of accurate dimension. In this section, I'll show you the best approaches for making a variety of straight cuts to help you with ripping and

THE RIPPING/RESAWING REDUNDANCY

Ripping **means sawing** parallel to the grain. But so does *resawing*. So what's the difference? Well, not much, really. Resawing is simply a form of ripping that generally refers to slicing a board through its thickness while standing it on its edge. Work is generally resawn to create anything from thin sheets of veneer to door panels. Don't let the terms confuse you. The saw and fence setup for ripping and resawing are virtually the same. The only real difference is the type of blade used (see Section 3) and perhaps the height of the fence. The main rule of thumb to remember is that a blade should have no fewer than 3 teeth for every inch of stock thickness.

As a rule of thumb, never use a blade that has fewer than 3 teeth per inch of stock thickness.

crosscutting, as well as approaches for sawing tapers, bevels, tenons, and other maneuvers.

Setting Up for Ripping

For straight, accurate ripping, a bandsaw must be outfitted with the appropriate blade for the job, and the blade guides and table must be correctly aligned. Depending on the particular operation, you may also need to set up a fence and adjust for saw drift.

Proper Blade

The first consideration when setting up a bandsaw for ripping is the type and size blade to use. Complete information on choosing blades is available in Section 3, but I'll recap here the fundamentals on blades used for ripping.

Ripping wood creates lots of stringy fibers that need to be efficiently evacuated from the saw cut via the blade gullets. Big gullets —found on blades with fewer teeth per inch—transport the sawdust most effectively. However, blades with fewer teeth may cut too aggressively for the particular thickness of stock being sawn. Remember that a blade should have no fewer than 3 teeth per 1-in. thickness of wood. Fewer teeth typically

See *"Tpi and Material Thickness"* on p. 59.

result in a rougher cut, a wider kerf, and a higher incidence of harmonic blade flutter.

Don't use an aggressive blade simply to get the work done more quickly. In fact, as long as its gullets are large enough to evacuate the sawdust, a blade with a few more teeth may cut better and faster because smaller teeth create less vibration. For example, ripping 4/4 hardwood with a 6-tpi hook-tooth

Even a narrow blade can produce accurate, consistent rips when properly set up. Here, a ¼-in. hook-tooth, 6-tpi blade creates translucent slices from 4/4 maple.

When ripping, the thrust guides provide the predominant blade support. As shown here, the operation proceeds fine even with the side bearings moved far from the blade.

blade creates an accurate cut with a decent edge. I typically use a wide blade for ripping because of its inherently increased beam strength, but even a narrow blade can do a good job when set up correctly.

[TIP] Dirt and detritus on roughsawn boards can dull blades. Brush, blow off, or vacuum dirty stock before sawing.

Guides

As discussed at length in Section 2, proper blade operation depends on accurately set blade guides. For ripping, the adjustment of the thrust guides is particularly important. If they are not coplanar to each other, the blade will try to twist, resulting in a wandering cut. The saw frame and guidepost must also be rigid enough to prevent the thrust bearings from deflecting under feed pressure.

Side guides should also be set up accurately, although they're not nearly as important as the thrust guides for ripping. As the photo

above right shows, even a narrow ¼-in., 6-tpi blade can do a great job of ripping without relying on the side guides, as long as the thrust bearings are accurately set and the blade is sharp.

[TIP] A finely tuned bandsaw with a sharp blade shouldn't be used as the shop scrap-cleanup saw.

Using Fences

A bandsaw fence can be used to guide work-pieces to make straight cuts and to efficiently create multiples of the same width or (in the case of resawing) thickness. There are two basic types of bandsaw fence: straight and single point.

A straight fence is used much like a table-saw fence, but with a twist of sorts. That is, a straight fence on a bandsaw must often be adjusted to accommodate blade drift, as explained in the sidebar on the facing page. When set up properly, a straight fence yields straight-edged workpieces of consistent width and resawn panels and veneers of consistent thickness.

A single-point fence—often simply a pointed block or round bar attached to the rip fence—is ideal for ripping shaped stock. The "point" serves as a fulcrum that allows steering the workpiece to follow the cut line while maintaining a consistent distance from the blade. However, a single-point fence will not produce pieces as consistently wide or thick as you can get when using a properly aligned straight fence.

Many commercial fences are available for bandsaws, but you can also make your own for general or specialized purposes. For example, you can easily make an L-shaped auxiliary fence for ripping narrow strips of thin stock, as shown in the bottom photo at left. It serves as a standoff from the primary, taller fence to allow positioning the guides closer to the workpiece. For more versatility, you can cobble up a "hi-lo" fence that will serve as a standoff for ripping narrow pieces as well as a standard-height fence for general work or a tall fence for resawing. To attach featherboards, you can

A single-point fence allows ripping pieces of consistent width from curved or irregular stock.

An L-shaped auxiliary fence clamped to the main fence allows close placement of the guides to the stock when ripping narrow strips.

▶ DEALING WITH DRIFT

***Blade drift* is the tendency** of a blade to cut in a particular direction, which may not be parallel to the rip fence or the edge of the saw table. It's a common problem and can often be attributed to a dull blade, poorly adjusted guides, or a table that's not square to the blade. Blade drift is most troublesome when ripping or resawing using a fence, because the blade's preferred direction either causes the workpiece to move away from the fence or it pulls the blade inward toward the fence.

It's best to avoid the problem by using a fresh blade, perfectly adjusted guides, and a table that's aligned square to the blade. However, when that doesn't do the trick, you'll have to accommodate the drift as explained on pp. 117–118 in this section. I first try adjusting the blade tracking to solve the problem, as shown on p. 117. If that doesn't work, the final solution is to adjust the fence for drift, as explained on p. 118.

install T-track into a high fence to accept featherboard mounting screws.

▶ See *"Making a Hi-Lo Fence"* on p. 119.

[TIP] **For easier clamping of fences, epoxy wood blocking between the webbing on the underside of the saw table**.

Squaring Table to Blade

The final step in setting up for ripping is to make sure the table is square to the blade—both vertically and front to back. To adjust for vertical square, retract the side guides, raise the guidepost all the way, and hold a square against blade and table. Do this with every blade change and before committing

Fence-mounted featherboards help hold thin stock to the table for accurate, safe ripping.

Square the table to the blade vertically every time you change blades.

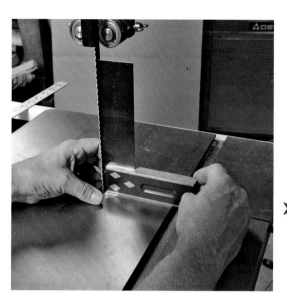

project wood to the blade. You never know when an inadvertent bump from heavy stock might have knocked the table askew.

Ideally, the front edge of the table should also be square to the blade. The blade's cutting path would then theoretically be parallel to a squarely set rip fence, which wouldn't have to be adjusted for blade drift.

▶ See *"Table"* on pp. 37–38.

Feeding Ripcuts

Cut quality depends to some degree on good feed technique. The two main concerns are direction and feed speed. Ideally, you want to feed straight on to the blade without applying any twist or sideways pressure that would cause the blade to deflect.

Feed speed affects both the cut-line accuracy and the quality of the cut surface. Overly aggressive feeding either slows the blade or clogs the gullets with sawdust, creating drag and power-sapping friction. Conversely, an unnecessarily slow feed rate denies the teeth constant bite, causing them to "hunt" for purchase and creating a rough edge in the process. An inconsistent fast-slow-fast-slow feed rate can produce harmonic blade vibration that results in an erratic cut line and a rippled surface.

The best approach is to feed the stock at a consistent, steady rate appropriate to the blade and the density and thickness of the wood being cut. The "proper" feed speed for a given workpiece isn't easily quantified, but you develop a feel for it with practice. Learn to listen to the saw while cutting at a steady rate. If the motor bogs down or the blade

PREVENTING BLADE FLEX

Constant forward pressure keeps the blade path straight.

When side pressure accompanies forward pressure, the blade tries to travel in multiple directions, forcing a crooked cut.

Guides

Blade

Guides

Blade

To help maintain a consistent feed rate, stand so your arms can handle the stock without major repositioning of your body.

starts to wander, ease up on the feed pressure. (You can't do much harm from cutting too slowly, except for wasting time.) To help with consistent feeding, stand at the saw so that your arms do the work with minimal body repositioning. It's smart to spend some time sawing scrap wood until you start to get a feel for the process.

[TIP] Bandsaw cuts are rougher on the bottom side. Saw with the "show" side of your stock facing upward.

Ripping Freehand

Freehand ripping doesn't utilize any fence or jig. You simply cut while following a scribed line. The technique is especially useful for cutting the occasional taper, ripping natural-edge or crooked stock, or doing any number of quick cuts where it's not really necessary to set up a fence or jig.

If I am cutting a single tenon or perhaps a few tenons of different dimensions, I'll often

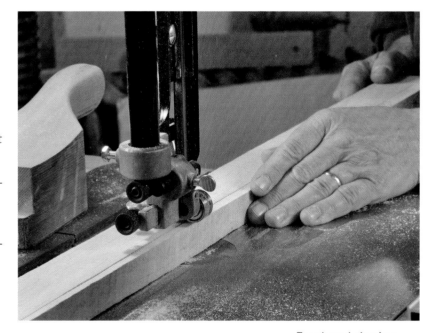

Freehand ripping eschews fences or other guides. You simply follow a scribed line by eye.

> ⚠ WARNING **When ripping a twisted board, maintain table contact at the blade. Keep your hands on top of the board to avoid pinching your fingers between the board and table**.

►TEST CUTS

Once you're satisfied that all the saw's adjustable parts are working in harmony, try a few test cuts on scrap material of a density and thickness similar to your project wood. Use clean stock without knots. It doesn't pay to dull the blade in the interest of saving a bit of wood. The test cuts will let you know how your adjustments fare. If you have a sharp, appropriate blade installed and it leads or drifts, it's time to recheck the guides, particularly the thrust bearings.

A straight fence set parallel to the blade's cut path ensures accurate, repeatable ripping of multiples.

forgo any fence or jig setup and cut them by eye. With practice and the correct blade, this is nearly as accurate as setting up a jig, and it saves lots of time. Keep in mind that free-hand ripping of boards on edge sometimes requires auxiliary support to keep the board perpendicular to the table.

Ripping with a Straight Fence

The use of a straight fence set parallel to the blade's cut path assures accurate ripping and resawing of same-size multiples. This is great for stock dimensioning, sawing veneers and stack laminations, and ripping tapers using a jig. A shopmade fence clamped to the table works fine, but a commercial fence can be quickly positioned and locked in place anywhere along the width of the table for efficient setups.

Orienting the Workpiece

When using a fence, you can choose to feed the workpiece with either the *keeper piece* or the *offcut* between the fence and the blade. The main advantage to feeding with the keeper piece between the fence and blade is that the fence doesn't have to be reset to cut multiple pieces of the same size. You can just refeed the board through again to cut another piece or begin with a new board. This is the most efficient way to cut multiples.

Unfortunately, this approach can be a bit troublesome when ripping multiple narrow strips. That's because the remainder of the board tends to tilt in toward the fence at the end of the cut, levering the last bit of the keeper piece away from the fence and creating a crooked cut at the end of the pass. It's also difficult to push the narrow keeper piece past the blade at the end of the cut.

When ripping narrow strips, the offcut section can pivot inward toward the fence, levering the strip (the keeper piece) away from the fence and causing a crooked cut at the end of the pass.

Ripping with the offcut section between the fence and blade means that the keeper piece is free to move away from the blade during and after the cut. This can be helpful when dealing with narrow offcuts or *reaction wood* that tends to spring away from the kerf. The biggest disadvantage to this approach is that, when cutting multiples, the

rip fence must be repositioned for each cut, which takes time and invites inaccuracies.

Ripping Multiples

Ripping multiple pieces of the same width is accomplished just like on a tablesaw: Simply set the fence to the desired width and rip away. Wide stock can easily be sawn into multiples by setting the fence the desired distance from the blade and then making repeated passes against the fence. Feeding the work with a push stick will keep it tight to the fence at the end of the cut, eliminating any tendency for it to move away from the fence, which would cause a curved cut at the end of the pass.

[TIP] When cutting multiples, saw setup is critical. Make sure the blade is cutting parallel to the fence before committing your project stock.

Rip narrow stock to the outside of the blade and follow the cut to the end with a sacrificial push stick.

A featherboard serves as a stop for ripping multiple thin strips from the outside edge of the board.

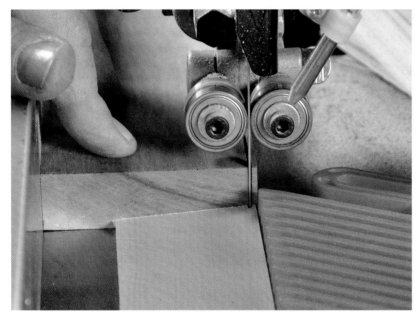

Use a sacrificial push stick to shove the stock past the blade at the end of the rip, reducing the possibility of a blade divot.

When ripping multiple narrow strips, I cut them from the edge of the board opposite the fence. I use a stiff featherboard as a stop, lightly placing the workpiece against the featherboard and then registering the fence against the workpiece before making the cut. The featherboard serves as a stop for each subsequent cut and also keeps the stock tight against the fence as the rip progresses. Alternatively, a single-point fence of some sort could be clamped to the table instead of a featherboard.

Ripping Narrow Pieces

I generally cut narrow pieces from the edge of the board opposite the fence, as described in the previous paragraph. Whether making one-off cuts or multiples, use a sacrificial push stick to move both the keeper piece and offcut past the blade's teeth. Stopping a narrow rip mid-cut can create a divot in the thin, flexible piece. Also, be sure to use a zero-clearance table insert to eliminate the possibility of the thin ripping slipping into the throat plate opening and possibly jamming the blade.

Ripping Thin Stock

Ripping thin boards requires a blade with a lot of teeth per inch. I suggest using a blade with at least 10 tpi for stock $\frac{3}{8}$ in. or thinner. For best results, use a regular-tooth blade. In order to place the upper blade guides close to the work, you'll need to either set up a low-profile fence or use an auxiliary "standoff" fence, as shown in the bottom photo at right.

▶ See *"Regular Tooth"* on p. 59.

It's often wise to set up fence-mounted featherboards to help hold thin stock tight to the table, especially on the outfeed side (see photo on p. 99). A zero-clearance table insert will help support thin stock at the point of cutting contact, reducing the chance of splitting the wood or getting a ragged cut.

Straight Cuts in Curved Stock

Ripping curved parts, such as stack-laminated drawer fronts or table aprons, can be safely accomplished with a bandsaw. The easiest approach is to work with the convex face of the work down. The important thing is to maintain contact between the stock and table right at the blade teeth. Use a moderately slow feed speed and a push stick to finish the cut. Don't reach around to pull the board through, because inadvertent

When ripping curved parts convex side down, make sure the part is securely supported by the table right at the blade.

side movement can cause the blade to catch on the stock.

When the geometry or finish side of a piece dictates sawing with the convex side up, use a support block at the blade that is tall enough to allow unimpeded feeding. Attach the block to a fence secured to the table with the blade buried in the block to ensure support at the point of blade entry.

When working with the convex side up, use a support block screwed to a tall fence, burying the blade in the block to provide support at the point of blade contact.

To rip a straight edge on a "live-edge" board, use double-face tape to attach a straight guide board to ride against the rip fence.

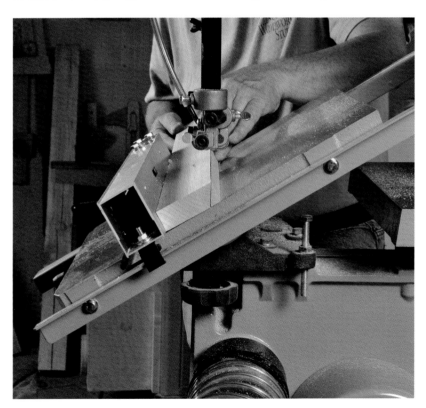

When ripping bevels, lock the fence to the table on the downhill side of the blade so that gravity helps keep the stock against the fence.

Ripping Live-Edge Material

Sawing a straight edge on a "live-edge" or waney board is easy. Simply attach a straight board to the top of the workpiece and run the straight edge against the saw fence. Double-face carpet tape works fine. Just make sure to clean dust from the contact surfaces so that the tape sticks securely. Screws or brads will work, too, but will leave holes in your stock.

Ripping Bevels

Straight bevel ripcuts are easily accomplished on the bandsaw. Most saws have tilting tables to accommodate angled cuts. Tilt the table to the desired angle and set your rip fence on the downhill side of the blade, letting gravity help you keep the stock tight to the fence.

Ripping Tapers

Tapers can be ripped freehand by following a scribed line, or you can use a taper jig for the job. A jig will typically produce a more uniform edge. One basic jigged approach is to use double-face tape to attach the workpiece at the desired angle to a guide board that rides along the rip fence. Alternatively, you can make more sophisticated taper jigs, such as those shown on pp. 123 and 124.

One type of jig, which incorporates "steps," can be used to make a variety of tapers of a specific angle. Or you can make an infinitely adjustable jig that can be used to make repeated tapers of just about any angle. Both of these jigs provide an easy way to make identical multiple tapers on the bandsaw.

One simple way to saw a taper is to attach the workpiece at the desired angle to a guide board that rides along the fence.

A grooved board serves as a sacrificial stabilizing cradle jig for ripping cylindrical stock.

Ripping Cylindrical Stock

Dowels, spindles, and other cylindrical workpieces require special support to prevent them from rolling during ripping. A cradle jig works well and can be made by simply plowing a groove or V-cut into one face of a sacrificial block, which is sawn along with the stock. The ripcut can be guided freehand or, if the sacrificial block is wide enough, fed against a rip fence. For a more precise approach, you can make a dedicated V-cradle with a kerf guide.

> See *"Cradle Jig for Cylindrical Stock"* on p. 128.

Ripping with a Single-Point Fence

The use of a single-point fence allows ripping curved and irregularly shaped stock into pieces of consistent width or thickness. Because the guiding surface is a projecting, rounded edge, you can steer the workpiece during the cut. This provides a great way to saw identical curved pieces to the same thickness without scribing a cutline.

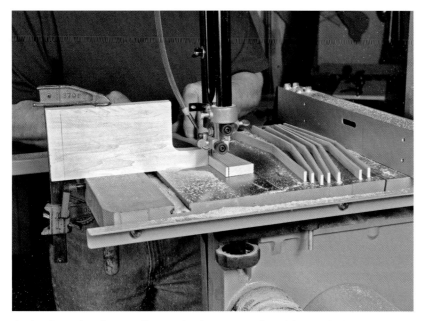

A single-point fence allows ripping curved and irregularly shaped pieces to identical thickness without the need for cut lines.

When resawing wide stock, a tall fence helps keep the workpiece square to the table to ensure a cut of consistent thickness.

When resawing, a single-point fence offers a quick setup alternative to adjusting a straight fence for bandsaw drift. Instead of adjusting the fence, you just work to a cut line gauged on the edge of the stock, correcting your course as necessary while you saw. A tall single-point fence ensures consistent thickness across the board while keeping it square to the table. Although quicker to set up, a single-point fence will not yield as smooth a surface nor as consistent a thickness as will a properly adjusted straight fence. Stock cleanup will also take longer, and more material will be lost in the cleanup process.

Resawing

Resawing means slicing a board across its width to create everything from veneer sheets to thin panels. The operation almost always involves straight cutting, and its accuracy depends upon absolutely coplanar thrust bearings, guides that won't deflect under heavy loads, and a sharp blade with big gullets to evacuate copious amounts of sawdust. It's also best to use a wide blade, which has more inherent beam strength than a narrow blade.

When resawing wide stock, a tall fence is essential to prevent the board from teetering on its edge and spoiling the cut. Use a push block to keep the board against the fence, but don't pinch the cut closed on the blade. Keep your feed pressure straight on to the blade.

Resawing often involves thick stock, which can suffer from drying imbalances. When sliced, improperly seasoned wood can immediately warp and pinch the blade. If that happens, insert a small wedge into

Resawing with an underpowered bandsaw can be made easier by first making some preliminary cuts with the tablesaw (seen here as the widely kerfed sections).

the kerf to keep it open and eliminate a blade bind.

Underpowered saws may strain to resaw thick stock. In that case, you can make some preliminary cuts on the tablesaw to make the job easier. By first cutting as deeply as you can with the tablesaw, you reduce the amount of wood the bandsaw must then slice through. (The disadvantage of this technique is that you waste more wood.) Make sure to use the widest blade your bandsaw will accept, because the guides will be a long way from the cutting action, which puts the blade's beam strength to the test.

[TIP] Due to their greater beam strength, wide blades are less prone to drift problems.

PUSH STICKS & PUSH BLOCKS

Push sticks and push blocks save stock as well as fingers. A push stick helps keep stock tight to the fence and table without putting your hands in harm's way. An all-around push stick can be something as simple as a scrap piece of wood with a notch cut in one end, such as the "fish stick" shown in the photo. The curve of its body places your hands in an advantageous spot, the notched mouth registers solidly at the end or edge of a board, and the flared tail offers a good hand grip.

You can also make a very useful push block, as shown on p. 112. It allows feeding workpieces past the end of the cut by letting you saw into the end of the block while providing clearance for the blade guides so that they can be set close to the workpiece.

A push stick is critical for safe work practices.

Tight butt joints can be cut on the band-saw using a wide, regular-tooth, high-tpi blade.

Setting Up for Crosscutting

A bandsaw can produce a cut straight and smooth enough to serve as a tight-fitting butt joint. Achieving this kind of accuracy simply requires the use of a fine-tooth blade suited to the stock thickness, as well as carefully adjusted blade guides and a table that's set precisely square to the blade.

Squaring the Table to the Blade

For accurate crosscutting, it's critical that the table is precisely square to the blade both vertically and horizontally. The vertical adjustment is necessary to ensure accurately perpendicular cuts, and the horizontal adjustment is necessary to ensure that the end of the piece is cut square to its edges.

Keep in mind that crosscuts are typically guided by a miter gauge that runs in the table slot. If the slot and blade path aren't parallel, a workpiece guided by the miter gauge won't approach the blade straight on,

which will result in a coarse, irregular cut. If your table doesn't have a slot, you can use a sled for the job, but it will also have to travel absolutely perpendicular to the blade for accurate crosscuts.

Using the Proper Blade

Almost any blade wider than 3/16 in. will work well for crosscutting. A wider blade tends to cut straighter, but narrow blades will work too, as long as the blade guides are set up accurately.

Crosscutting wood is a significantly different process than ripping wood. When crosscutting, the wood fibers are sheared crossways, producing tiny bits of waste rather than the long fibers created when ripping. This allows the use of a blade with smaller gullets. My favorite crosscut blade is a 1/2-in. 6-tpi regular-tooth blade. The wide blade body reduces flutter that causes rough cuts, and the regular tooth configuration easily evacuates the sawdust. A blade with even more teeth per inch will create a smoother cut yet, so use the highest-tpi blade possible when you want the smoothest cut.

Crosscutting with a Miter Gauge

Accurate crosscuts require feeding the wood in a path exactly in line with the blade's cutting path. A miter gauge, which runs in a slot machined in the saw table, is a great way to guide a workpiece for an accurate crosscut. A miter gauge can typically be adjusted to make crosscuts ranging from 90° to slightly more than 45°. Because the head of a miter gauge is relatively short, it's helpful to add a long fence to provide stability for the workpiece and to support it close to the blade. Length stops can be clamped or screwed to the long fence for repeatable cutting accuracy.

[TIP] If a board is too wide to conveniently push with the miter gauge, you can reverse the miter gauge and use it as a sort of steady rest, holding the piece against it as you push.

Crosscutting with a Sled

As an alternative to a miter gauge, you can use a shopmade crosscut sled, which offers additional advantages. Because the workpiece rides on the sled base as well as against the full-length fence, both the keeper piece and the offcut are supported throughout the cut. This helps reduce mistakes and works particularly well when cutting small workpieces. A sled is cheap and easy to make.

➤ See "A Crosscut Sled" on p. 127.

A miter gauge rides in the table slot and guides pieces into the blade for accurate crosscuts.

A simple, accurate crosscut sled can be cobbled together from a piece of plywood and a few hardwood scraps.

A

"FISH" PUSH STICK

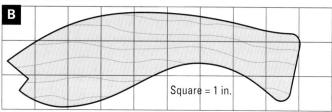

B

Square = 1 in.

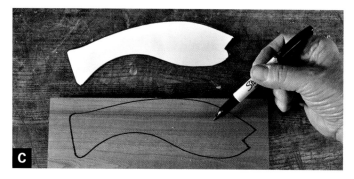

C

Making a "Fish" Push Stick

The "fish stick" is one of my favorite push sticks. Its curved body fits my hand well and keeps it at a safe distance above the cut line. The flare of the tail makes it easy to hold firmly, and the acute angle of the mouth provides a notch for pushing the wood around. The push stick is short enough to offer adequate safety margins while allowing good control of the stock (A).

Enlarge the pattern (B) and copy the full-size profile to a piece of ½-in.- or ¾-in.-thick wood or plywood (C). If using solid wood, make sure the grain runs the length of the stick. Short grain running across the body invites fracturing (D). Making the stick from plywood side steps that danger, but plywood isn't as nice to handle as solid wood.

Saw the profile (E), and then ease the edges with a four-in-hand rasp or rout them with a ³⁄₈-in. roundover bit for a more comfortable grip (F). A rare-earth magnet embedded in the side of the push stick will keep it handily stuck to your saw's wheel house door (G).

D

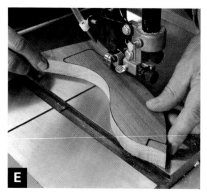

E

F

G

Making a Push Block

This push block allows you to push small or narrow pieces slightly past the end of the cut by actually sawing into the end of the block. The large notch in the end allows clearance for the blade guides so that they can be set close to the workpiece.

This pusher can be made from a scrap chunk of 4x4 stock. Its length not only keeps your hands a safe distance from the blade, but also offers long life for the push stick. When the end gets too sliced up from use, simply crosscut away the damaged area and you've got a fresh start. The angled handle makes it easy to put lateral and forward pressure on the stock at the same time.

Making the block involves compound sawing—forming the shape by cutting it out from two different profiles. This is basically the same approach used to make a cabriole leg. Begin by enlarging the patterns **(A)** to full size, and then use them to lay out a side and top profile on a 4x4 scrap **(B)**. Cut the side profile **(C)**, tape the offcuts back on **(D)**, and then cut the top profile **(E)**.

(continued on p. 114)

PUSH BLOCK

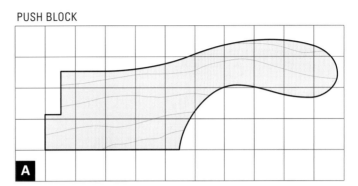

A

Side profile

Square = 1 in.

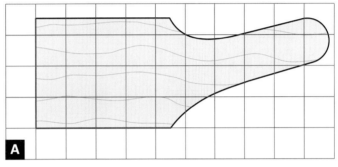

A

Top profile

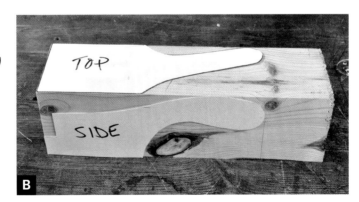

B

C

You now have the basic shape of the push block **(F)**. All that's left is to saw the notch and round the handle with a spokeshave and a rasp **(G)**. You now have a big ol' push block that offers control and safety for nearly every bandsaw ripping operation **(H)**.

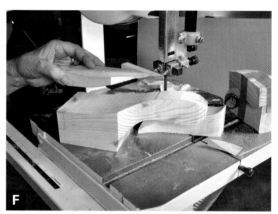

Freehand Ripping

Freehand straight-line ripping requires practice and good hand-eye coordination. Spend some time cutting scrap wood until you get a feel for it. Learn to anticipate the cutting path and to make slight steering corrections that prevent a wandering cut from getting out of hand. Once the general cut direction is established, it's pretty easy to keep it on track.

I typically steer the cut and push the workpiece with my right hand while my left hand acts as an infinitely adjustable fence **(A)**. Start the cut slowly, maneuvering the workpiece with both hands until the blade is following the cutline without the need for major steering corrections. Once the cut is established, rest the fingers of your left hand on the bandsaw table, using your middle finger as a guidepost and your index finger as a hold-down **(B)**. Continue the cut, keeping your left hand stationary while your right hand makes any steering corrections necessary to stay on the cutline.

Any corrections you make should be very minor. If you find yourself making large swings, check your blade guides for proper adjustment. If they seem correctly aligned, you may be using a damaged or dull blade. Keep in mind that sometimes a knot or other change in the wood's density can cause a blade to go off course.

When you near the end of the cut, reposition your left hand on the back side of the cut **(C)** and finish the cut by either pulling the board through with both hands to the rear of the blade or using a push stick with your right hand to follow through **(D)**.

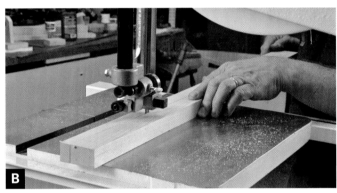

Cutting a 3-Sided Notch

Bandsawing accurate, straight-sided notches is relatively easy. Start by sawing both sides of the notch down to the baseline. Use a miter guide for straight, accurate cuts **(A)**. Now, saw diagonally from one corner to the other, curving the line as much as the blade will allow **(B)**. With the waste removed, cut as close to the baseline as possible, curving downward into the opposite corner **(C)**. Finish the notch by laying the blade against the baseline and returning the cut to the opposite corner **(D)**, creating a straight, accurate baseline with crisp, 90° corners **(E)**.

Blade Tracking for Drift Adjustment

If your bandsaw has crowned tires, you can try eliminating blade drift using a blade-tracking trick devised by Canadian woodworker Michael Fortune. By adjusting the position of the blade on its tire crown, he essentially aligns it parallel to the sides of the table. Here's how to approach it.

Start by scribing a line parallel to the edge of a piece of straight stock. To determine the blade drift, rip the stock while carefully following the line **(A)**. A blade that's precisely centered on the tire crown should have no drift angle and should cut perfectly parallel to the sides of the saw table **(B)**. If the blade is tracking forward of the crown, the teeth will be angled slightly inward, creating a cut that drifts away from the fence (with the fence to the left of the blade). For accurate ripping, one approach would be to angle the fence toward the right-hand side of the table **(C)**. Conversely, if the blade is tracking off the back of the crown, it tends to point the teeth outward, resulting in a cut that moves toward a squarely set fence. In this case, you could angle the fence toward the left-hand side of the table to accommodate the drift **(D)**. (Adjusting a fence for drift is described in more detail in the following photo essay.)

The problem with adjusting the fence angle is that it doesn't help with accurate crosscutting, which requires the table slot to be parallel to the blade as well. Fortune's approach is to track the blade as necessary to align its cutting path with the table slot. That way, the rip fence can be aligned to the slot, and the cutting angle will remain parallel to the fence as well as to the table slot **(E)**. This may require a number of test cuts, but once it's set up, you'll be primed for accurate ripping *and* crosscutting. The evidence will be a blade that's visually centered in its kerf **(F)**. I've had some success with this method, but I have to admit that it's not always successful.

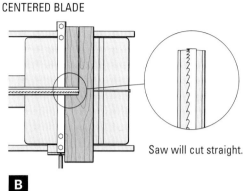

CENTERED BLADE

Saw will cut straight.

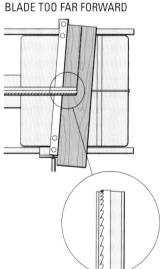
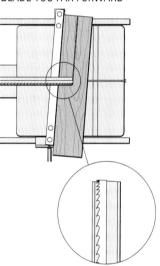
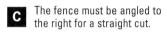

BLADE TOO FAR FORWARD

BLADE TOO FAR BACK

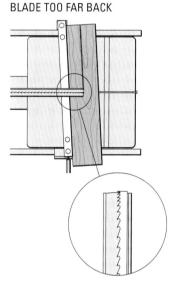

C The fence must be angled to the right for a straight cut.

D The fence must be angled to the left for a straight cut.

ALIGN THE BLADE JUST ONCE

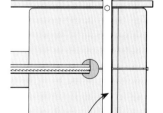

E Align the rip fence parallel with the miter gauge slot.

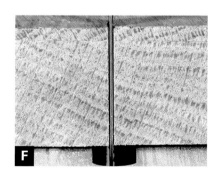

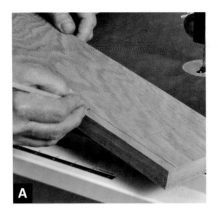

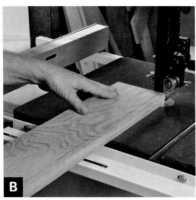

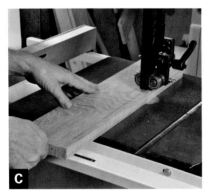

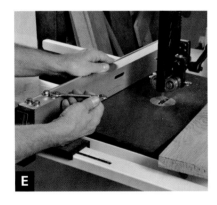

Adjusting a Fence for Drift

Begin by moving your upper guides to within ¼ in. of the height of the material you plan to rip/resaw. Check your thrust bearings to make sure they are correctly positioned and securely set.

Next, establish the drift angle using a test piece of lumber that's similar in density and thickness to the stock you want to cut. Joint one edge, scribe a line parallel to it **(A)**, and saw to the line. Start slowly and carefully **(B)**, but as the cut is established, increase the feed speed. Once a steady, straight feed pattern is established, continue sawing until the test board nears the far edge of the table **(C)**. Stop sawing, and hold the board securely in place while you shut off the machine.

After the blade has stopped, scribe a pencil line on the saw table along the fence edge of the board **(D)**. Be careful not to move the board while scribing along it. Align your rip fence to the scribed line and carefully lock the fence angle in place **(E)**. A commercial fence that rides on rails will maintain this drift angle regardless of its position on the rails **(F)**. To set up a shopmade fence that clamps to the table, you'll have to measure over from your penciled drift reference line. Try a test rip before committing project stock **(G)**. If your setup is correct, the board will not wander away from the fence, and the blade will not wander toward the fence.

[VARIATION] When making the initial cut to determine drift direction in tall stock, use a shopmade support to keep the board perpendicular to the table as you cut.

Making a Hi-Lo Fence

A hi-lo fence is one of the simplest and most useful jigs you can make for your bandsaw. The three-piece unit can be configured for use as a standoff for ripping narrow strips **(A)**, a standard-height fence for general work **(B)**, or a tall fence for resawing **(C)**.

The jig consists of a base (the standoff section), the fence, and the fence riser **(D)**. The fence is screwed to the base and hinged to the riser. Powerful rare-earth magnets inset into the edges of the fence and riser hold the two pieces together vertically when in use as a tall fence.

Begin by making the fence and riser from ³⁄₄-in.-thick plywood. Then connect the two pieces with inexpensive hinges. No need to mortise them into the edges or even screw them into place. I simply nail them to the rear faces of the parts **(E)**. With the parts folded against each other, mark across the edges with a square to lay out mating blind holes for ⅛-in.-thick x ¼-in.-dia. rare-earth magnets. (See Resources on p. 198.) After drilling the ⅛-in.-deep holes, install magnets into them **(F)**. (I use fast-drying glue for the job.)

Make the base from ½-in.-thick plywood or solid wood, and then drill and countersink it for attachment to the bottom of the fence. Finish up the jig by screwing the base to the fence, making sure both pieces are set carefully flush to each other **(G)**.

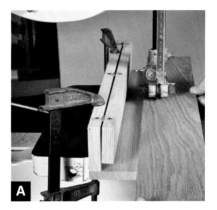
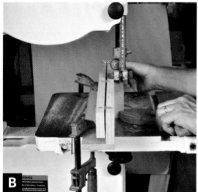
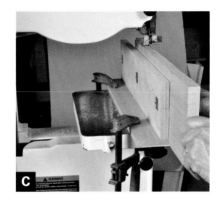
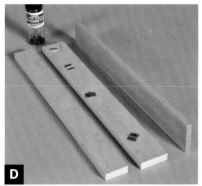
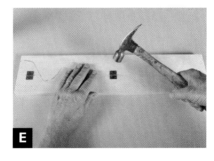

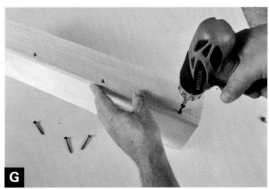

A

SINGLE-POINT FENCE

3/8-in. radius round-over

Nose piece support (3/4 in. x 3 1/4 in. x 6 in.)

2 1/2-in. x 1/4-in.-dia. NC hex bolt

5-star knob with 1/4-in. NC thread

1/4-in.-dia. washer

A

3/4 in.

1/4-in.-dia. washer

1 3/8 in.

5/16-in.-dia. hole centered on width, 3 in. from end

5-star knob with 1/4-in. NC thread

1 3/8 in.

Base (3/4 in. x 6 in. x 15 in.)

A: See "Layout for Nose Pieces"

Size runner to fit table slot.

Inset 2 1/2-in. x 1/4-in.-dia. NC hex bolt into bottom of base.

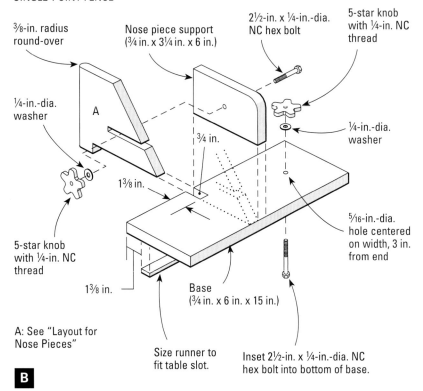

B

Making a Single-Point Fence

I designed my single-point fence for easy adjustability. Its base is guided by a runner in the table slot that allows front-to-back jig placement, while the jig's nose piece can be adjusted in or out relative to the blade **(A)**. The jig consists of four basic parts: the base, its runner, the nose, and the nose support. I also made a couple of extra nose pieces to suit workpieces of different heights, which allows for setting the guides close to the workpiece. For storage convenience, I attach the extra nose pieces to the jig with a knob. All the parts on my jig are made from 3/4-in.-thick hardwood plywood and solid maple **(B)**.

Start with the plywood base, making it 6 in. wide by the length of the table. Add a hardwood runner that fits your table slot without sideways slop. Position it so the edge of the base sits 2 in. back from the blade. Saw the notch in the plywood to accommodate the front section of the nose piece.

Next, make the nose pieces. The most efficient approach is to first glue 3/4-in. by 1-in. strips of dense hardwood to opposing edges of a 10-in.-square piece of plywood. Plane the edges flush to the plywood **(C)**, and then rout both sides of the strips using a 3/8-in. roundover bit to create the nosing **(D)**. Lay out the nose pieces as shown

C

D

in the drawing (E), and then cut out their profiles. Next, carefully notch out the bottom of each nose piece (F). It's critical that the bottom and front edges are precisely square to each other to ensure that the nose sits parallel to the bandsaw blade. Check the setup with a square (G).

Lay out and cut the adjustment slot on each nose piece after drilling a 5/16-in.-dia. hole 3 in. back from the bearing edge (H). Make the nose support and drill it at the center to accept a 5/16-in. x 2-in. machine bolt that aligns with the slot you cut in the nose pieces. Screw the nose support to the base, in line with the notch you previously cut (I). You can now attach your chosen nose piece to its support with a lock knob. As a final touch, I countersunk the underside of the base to accept a bolt for attaching the extra nose pieces when not in use (J).

[TIP] I use hex bolts for my jigs because carriage bolt heads eventually spin out. A bit of glue will usually keep a hex head bolt from turning.

SINGLE-POINT FENCE NOSE PIECES

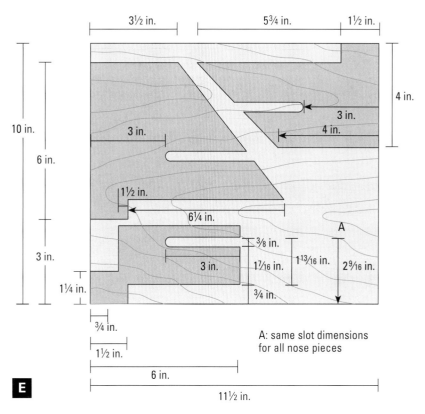

A: same slot dimensions for all nose pieces

E

F

G

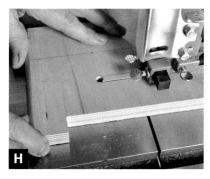

H

I

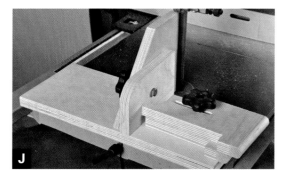

J

Setting Up a Single-Point Fence

For a single-point fence to work correctly, the apex of the nose piece must sit just slightly forward of the blade's teeth. This ensures that the workpiece establishes firm contact with the fence immediately before the blade touches the wood. Drawing a line down the apex of the nose aids the initial setup.

With the jig sitting in its table slot, register a square against the edge of the table with its blade touching the jig's nose, and mark the point of intersection **(A)**. Next, set the square upright on the table and gauge a line fully down the center of the nose **(B)**. Use the line to set the apex of the nose about ⅟₁₆ in. in front of the blade teeth **(C)**. The setup should produce cuts of consistent thickness **(D)**.

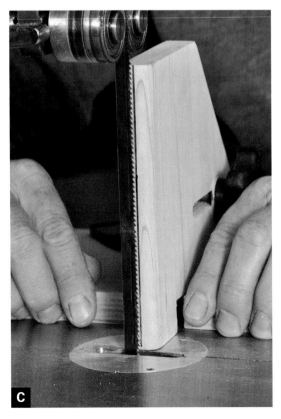

A Basic Taper Jig

A simple jig for cutting a specific variety of tapers can be made from a piece of plywood notched in ¼-in. increments. Although the jig is somewhat limiting, and workpieces longer than 24 in. can be a bit unwieldy to handle on the short bandsaw table, it can be made from scrap in just a few minutes and will produce accurate tapers.

Start with a piece of hardwood plywood at least 6 in. longer than the workpiece and at least 4½ in. wide in order to provide sufficient feeding clearance between fence and guides. Lay out the ¼-in. x ¼-in. steps, beginning about 1 in. in from one end **(A)**. Saw a stop cut at the innermost increment, and then rip the long section. Finish up by sawing out the remaining steps **(B)**.

Using the Basic Taper Jig

To use the basic taper jig, simply hold the work-piece against the edge of the jig with the narrow end of the taper seated in whichever notch provides the correct taper **(A)**. (If it helps, you can draw the complete taper on your first piece for setup purposes.) Set the saw fence for the desired cut width at the wide end of the work-piece, allowing a bit extra for cleanup afterward.

Feed the stock forward, keeping it tight against the jig **(B)**. If the taper begins on the side of the workpiece rather than at the end, start the cut slowly while allowing the blade to fully engage in the cut before increasing feed speed. As the cut progresses, reach around to the rear of the saw to keep the stock tight to the jig **(C)**. The fin-ished part should have a nice, straight taper that requires only a few passes with a handplane to smooth the sawn surface **(D)**.

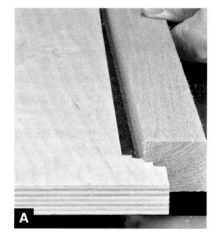

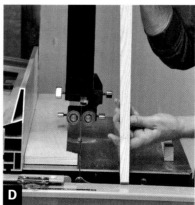

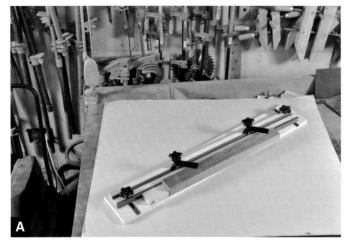

A

B

C

Adjustable Taper Jig

This tapering jig allows infinite adjustment for cutting just about any taper you like. The jig consists of three basic parts: the base, the fence, and a stop block. In addition, it's outfitted with commercial hold-downs that provide safety and ensure cut accuracy. All of the parts connect to each other with bolts inserted in T-tracks, providing infinite fine adjustability **(A)**.

The jig can be used on either side of the blade and, because of the movable stop, the cut can be approached from either end instead of having to start it on the wide end of the workpiece. This is especially useful when making partial tapers that don't extend the full length of the workpiece.

Make the jig a bit longer than the longest taper you plan to cut. Mine has a 38-in.-long base and a 36-in.-long fence, which is big enough to make 31-in. table legs. The 6-in.-wide base allows adequate clamping surface and provides good clearance for the bandsaw guides. The parts can be made from solid hardwood or plywood. This particular jig has a plywood base and stop block. The fence is made from hard maple.

Start by making the base. After sawing it to size, crosscut a ⅜-in.-deep x ¾-in.-wide dado 2 in. in from each end. Cut two pieces of ⅜-in.-thick T-track to the proper length and screw them into the dadoes **(B)**.

Next, make the ¾-in. x 2½-in. fence. Plow a ⅜-in.-deep x ¾-in.-wide groove down the center of the face to accept the T-track. Cut one length of ⅜-in.-thick T-track and one length of ½-in.-thick T-track the full length of the fence. Install the former in the groove and the latter along the edge **(C)**.

Create the holes for the fence attachment knobs. Because the fence is angled in use, one of its ends must be slotted to allow the necessary movement. Drill a couple of ⁵⁄₁₆-in.-dia. holes at one end of the track, as shown in the drawing **(D)**. (One or the other of these holes may prove more convenient for a particular operation.) Then make a ⁵⁄₁₆-in.-wide slot at the other end of the fence. You can rout the slot or drill and chop it out **(E)**.

Make the stop block, and then saw or rout one edge of it to create a ¹⁄₈-in.-long tongue that slides easily in the T-track slot **(F)**. Finish up by drilling a ¹⁄₄-in.-dia. hole through the width of the stop for mounting it to the T-track using a ¹⁄₄-in. x 3-in. bolt. Secure the block with a washer and wing nut.

ADJUSTABLE TAPER JIG

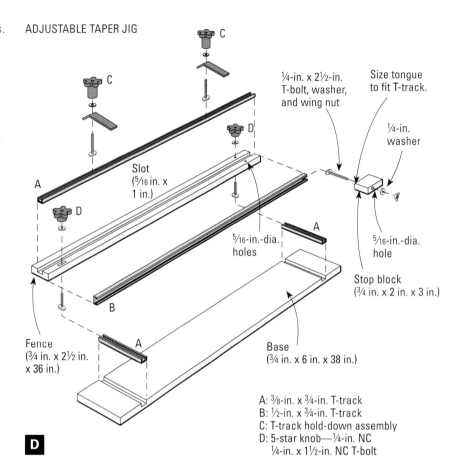

¹⁄₄-in. x 2¹⁄₂-in. T-bolt, washer, and wing nut

Size tongue to fit T-track.

¹⁄₄-in. washer

Slot (⁵⁄₁₆ in. x 1 in.)

⁵⁄₁₆-in.-dia. holes

⁵⁄₁₆-in.-dia. hole

Stop block (¾ in. x 2 in. x 3 in.)

Fence (¾ in. x 2¹⁄₂ in. x 36 in.)

Base (¾ in. x 6 in. x 38 in.)

A: ³⁄₈-in. x ¾-in. T-track
B: ¹⁄₂-in. x ¾-in. T-track
C: T-track hold-down assembly
D: 5-star knob—¼-in. NC
   ¼-in. x 1¹⁄₂-in. NC T-bolt

D

E

F

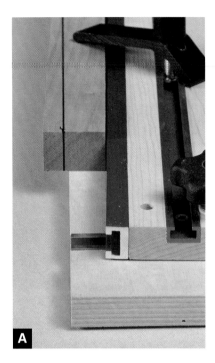

A

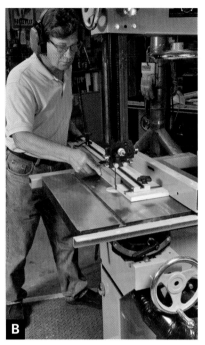

B

Using the Adjustable Taper Jig

Draw the desired taper on the workpiece, and then mount it on the jig with the cut line extended out from the jig base by about ⅛ in **(A)**. This will prevent cutting into the jig itself. Make sure the stop is firmly locked in place against the end of the stock, and then clamp the workpiece to the jig with hold-downs mounted in their T-tracks. Use fairly light clamp pressure. Overdoing it can pull the fence off the base.

Set your rip fence after adjusting it for drift if necessary. Then start sawing slowly **(B)**. Once the cut is established, maintain a steady feed rate **(C)**, reaching around the guidepost to keep the jig tight to the fence as the cut progresses **(D)**.

C

D

A Crosscut Sled

This crosscut sled is an improvement over a standard miter gauge because it carries both halves of a cut workpiece securely past the blade. It's also safer because the blade is buried in the fence at the end of the cut. It makes for very accurate cuts, especially when working with small pieces or irregularly shaped parts.

In preparation for making the sled, mark the blade's path on the bandsaw table. Then remove the blade. Make a hardwood runner about 6 in. longer than the table, fitting it snugly into the table slot. To ensure accurate crosscutting, the runner should slide easily, but without side-to-side play **(A)**.

Now make the base from ¾-in.-thick hardwood plywood. (Mine is 22 in. wide x 11 in. deep.) Position it on the table over the runner so the saw cut will be centered along the width of the plywood and square to the bandsaw table **(B)**. Carefully transfer the location of the runner onto the underside of the base **(C)**, and then screw the runner in place **(D)**.

Make and attach a ¾-in.-thick x 1½-in.-high hardwood fence about 5 in. back from the leading edge of the base **(E)**. It's important that the fence be straight. Set it further back if you intend to crosscut wide lumber, but leave enough meat to avoid weakening the base once it's kerfed. Again, make sure the fence is square to the bandsaw table. Add a 6-in.-long piece of wood to the rear of the fence, centering on the cut. This backstop serves as a reinforcing blade guard of sorts, allowing you to completely bury the blade in the fence for safety without sacrificing fence strength.

Mount the sled and check for smooth sliding action along the length of the table slot. Then reinstall the blade and carefully cut a slot up to the fence **(F)**. When cutting small pieces, feel free to bury the blade in the backstop for safety **(G)**.

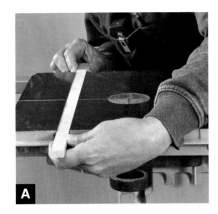
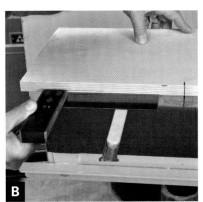
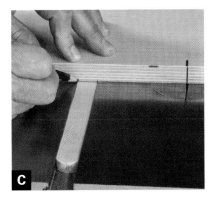
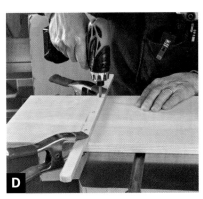

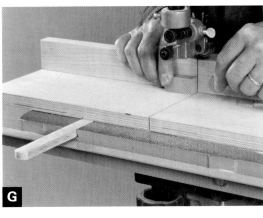

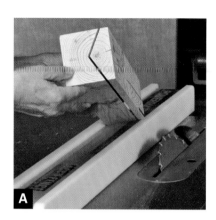

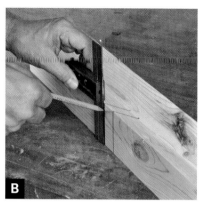

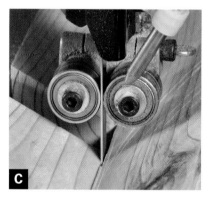

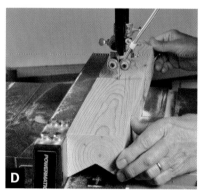

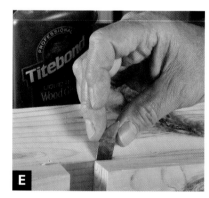

Cradle Jig for Cylindrical Stock

Sawing cylindrical stock can be dicey if it isn't properly supported. Freehand ripping of dowels and spindles is hard to do accurately, and freehand crosscutting of the same can cause a workpiece to spiral out of control. This easy-to-make cradle jig will accurately and safely guide cylindrical stock of all sorts. When ripping, a splitter at the center of the cradle keeps the stock from rotating. When crosscutting, the pressure of holding the workpiece against the walls of the cradle prevents the piece from spinning.

I typically make a jig like this from lumberyard 4x4 material. It should be at least 20 in. long to provide adequate support on either side of the blade. Begin by cutting the V-channel on the table saw with the blade set at a 30° angle. Make sure the two mating cuts meet cleanly at their apex **(A)**. Lay out a 1-in.-wide notch halfway down the jig, extending from the edge to the bottom of the V **(B)**. This provides access for the blade when ripping. Saw out the notch, set the bandsaw fence to center the blade in the cradle, and cut a kerf ¾ in. down the center of the V **(C)**. Flip the cradle upside down and end-for-end, and repeat the kerf cut at the other end of the blade access notch **(D)**. One kerf houses the blade during the cut, and the other holds a splitter, which you can make from wood, copper, or aluminum. I typically fix the splitter in place with hide glue, which can easily be softened with water or heat if it needs replacing **(E, F)**.

When ripping, you can either clamp the cradle to the table or mount it to the rip fence. I prefer the latter, which makes setup a breeze **(G)**. When crosscutting, guide the cradle with a miter gauge, holding the workpiece firmly in place. Extend the workpiece off the end of the cradle near the blade **(H)**.

Sawing
Basic Curves

Circles and Arcs

Complex Curves

- Arc Layout with String (p. 150)
- Arc Layout Using a Flexible Strip (p. 151)
- Two-Board Arc Layout (p. 152)
- Using a Beam Compass (p. 153)
- Making a Beam Compass (p. 154)
- A Basic Circle-Cutting Jig (p. 155)
- Using a Basic Circle-Cutting Jig (p. 156)

- Making a Curve Template (p. 157)
- Using a Curve Template (p. 158)
- String Layout for Ellipse (p. 159)
- Creating a Symmetrical Oval (p. 160)

CURVES LEND ELEGANCE, strength, and comfort to woodworking projects. Curved parts can constitute important design elements in everything from chairs, tables, and cabinets to architectural woodwork. When it comes to cutting curves, there is no other power tool in the shop that can compete with a bandsaw.

Bandsawn curves can be made free-hand or by using templates, fences, or jigs. Freehand cutting offers the ability to follow scribed lines and patterns as well as to cut compound curves. Templates allow accurate replication of curved pieces. Circle-cutting jigs can create accurately round circles of any dimension desired, and fences provide for repeatable cuts of accurate dimension.

The bandsaw can make accurate, smooth curved cuts, but it won't do it automatically. In this section I'll show you how to set up and use your bandsaw to make a variety of basic curved cuts. In Section 8, I'll address cutting complex curves.

Laying Out Circles and Arcs

It's nearly impossible to lay out an accurate circle freehand. And many curves consist of arcs, which are technically segments of a circle's circumference. As a result, it can be difficult to lay out smooth, fair curves freehand. But it's easily accomplished with a number of different drawing tools, including compasses, circle templates, adjustable arc templates, and even computer programs.

Using the proper tools, you don't have to employ a lot of math to lay out circles and arcs. Just remember that the radius of a circle is a line between its center and any point on its circumference. A circle's diameter is its width, which is twice the radius. To draw a circle or arc of a given size, you can simply set a compass to the desired radius and draw with that.

Compasses

The easiest way to lay out accurate circles is with a compass. A compass is comprised of a pair of legs that are hinged at one end to allow their spread at the opposite end. A compass typically has a locating point on one leg, which serves as a pivot, and a pencil or scribe point on the other. Most compasses can be set securely to a desired radius for laying out accurately repeatable curves. A drafting compass will work well for circles and arcs less than about 14 in. in diameter.

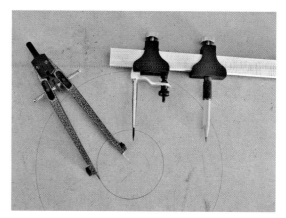

The drafting compass on the left works well for smaller circles, while the beam compass on the right can be expanded to create a circle of nearly any diameter.

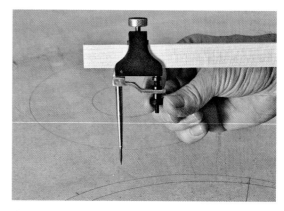

One of the trammel heads on a good-quality beam compass usually includes a micro-adjust for fine-tuning the desired radius.

Beam compasses offer the ability to scribe circles larger than those made by a drafting compass. A beam compass typically consists of two trammel heads attached to a shopmade hardwood or metal beam of any desired length. Economy trammel head sets usually consist of a pair of very basic scribe points. On better sets, one trammel head includes a micro-adjust for fine-tuning the radius, and the second head features

Large arcs and circles can easily be scribed using a beam compass.

an interchangeable holder to accommodate either a pencil or a scribe point.

To set a beam compass, you adjust the distance between the trammel heads to yield the desired radius and then lock them in place on the beam. To lay out an arc or circle, locate one trammel point at the center of the circle and rotate the other point (or pencil) around it.

A beam compass is great for laying out long arcs for, say, a decorative wooden valance. To set the beam compass, you'll need to know the radius of the arc. No problem. As long as you know the length and height of the arc, you can use the equation in the drawing at right to find the radius.

[TIP] **Metal is the best material to use for very long beams, as long wood pieces may tend to flop a bit.**

FINDING THE RADIUS OF AN ARC

To set a compass for drawing an arc, you need to know its radius. To determine the radius from the arc's height and length, use the following equation:

$$r = \frac{4h2 + L2}{8h}$$

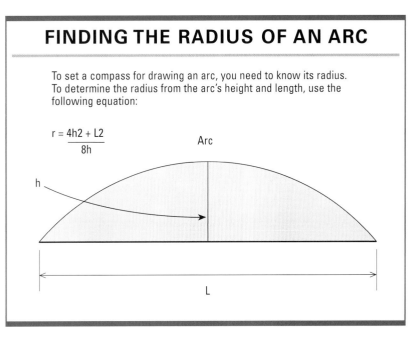

Arc

h

L

The terms *template* and *pattern* are often used interchangeably. However, patterns are technically the original designs from which templates are created. Patterns represent a particular shape, while templates are the tools used to make the shape in your chosen material. Patterns are typically produced on paper, making them easy to store, duplicate, and electronically transmit. A pattern can be glued to the project material or used for tracing a cut line, while a template serves to directly guide a saw, router, or other tool. Templates for woodworking are typically constructed from plywood, hardboard, or plastic and are held to the workpiece with double-face tape, brads, or small screws. Templates can also be used as scribing patterns for tracing outlines with a pen or pencil.

Circle templates provide a quick way of scribing small, accurate circles.

circles or laying out arcs of definite length. These templates are ideal for marking off rounded corners on project parts and connecting arcs or other curves without the use of a compass.

Adjustable Arc Template
Patented by James Hoyle in 1957, the Acu-Arc™ adjustable arc template can be set to describe arcs with radii as small as 7 in. up to radii of about 200 in. A centerline on the template provides an easy means of centering the arc, and it can also be used to determine the centerline or center point of an existing curve.

By using the centerline and arc end demarcations on the guide, an arc can be accurately continued beyond the length of the template. The guide makes easy work of drawing arcs with large radii without the need for a beam compass or the space needed to use one. It is also handy for determining the radius of a known arc. For example, to find the radius of a curved chair back, simply form the template to the part and the

Circle Templates
Circle templates are plastic sheets with round cutouts for scribing small circles of accurate sizes. Available from art or office supply dealers, they come in a variety of diameter ranges, with the largest circle typically about 3½ in. The edges of the openings are marked in increments to aid in centering

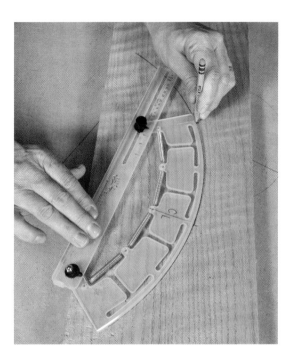

The Acu-Arc adjustable arc template will quickly and accurately produce or determine an arc of almost any diameter.

scale will give you the exact radius without requiring any math.

Computer-Generated Patterns

Computer-aided drafting (CAD) programs can quickly and accurately describe arcs, circles, and complex curves. The resulting drawings can be broken into printer-size sections that can be taped together to make patterns for creating templates or for affixing directly to the piece to serve as a cut line.

Laying Out Variable Curves

Boat builders have long used the term *fair curve* to describe an accurate curve that doesn't suffer from lumps, bumps, or flat spots. A correctly set-up bandsaw and good sawing technique will go a long way toward cutting a fair curve, but if the original layout is sloppy, the resulting curve will be less than

fair. Nice, fair variable curves can be laid out using curve templates, splines, and other tools designed for the purpose.

French Curves

French curves are standard drawing aids for architects, artists, designers, and furniture makers. A French curve is simply a template, usually made of clear plastic, that is composed of curves of many different radii blending smoothly in a variety of appealing arcs. It is used to draw a smooth line through existing points to create smooth transitions between circles or straight lines in a design. It also works well for refining hand-drawn curves or variable curves that aren't true arcs.

French curves create smooth transition lines between existing points.

French curves are typically sold in sets of two or three different templates that will cover a large variety of sweeps of different sizes and shapes. Look for sets that include large French curves, which are the most useful for furniture work.

Drawing Splines & Flexible Curves

Drawing splines are adjustable curves made of multiple interlocking plastic strips that slide along each other as the spline bends along its length. The strips always form a fair curve, which will provide a smooth transition when a line changes radius or direction. A spline can be used as a drawing guide to connect a series of points or to copy an existing curve. It's available in several different lengths, but I've found the 48-in.-long version to be the most versatile around the

Lead-filled flexible curves work well for transferring a known curve to a pattern.

shop. It's plenty long for most jobs, and it will form an arc as tight as 6 in. in diameter. Shorter-length splines are narrower and can make even tighter turns.

Another tool for transferring a curve to a pattern is called a *flexible curve*. These lead-cored plastic strips will bend to conform to any curved shape—regular or irregular. Flexible curves kink too easily for designing fair curves, but they work well for transferring them.

Profile Gauge

A profile gauge resembles a fine-toothed comb with the teeth pressed tightly against each other and projecting from either side of a friction-fit holding bar. Great for copying existing shapes and curves, profile gauges can quickly produce accurate patterns of complex or irregular shapes. When pressed against an irregular object, the teeth slide to conform to the surface of the object, holding an accurate pattern to trace. They're available in various lengths with metal or plastic teeth. I prefer plastic.

A drawing spline can be used to create smooth curves between established points.

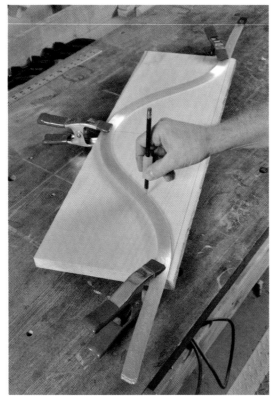

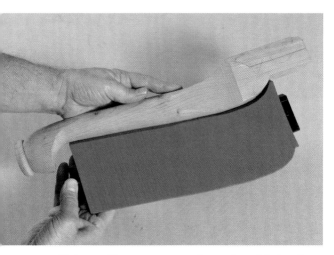

This profile gauge consists of multiple plastic teeth that slide to conform to irregular shapes and curves.

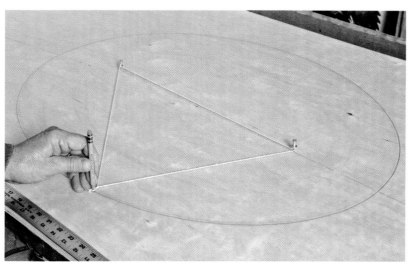

Two nails, a piece of string, and a pencil are all that's needed to draw accurate ellipses.

Ellipses & Ovals

Ellipses and ovals are two slightly different geometric shapes. An ellipse is an oblique, symmetrical slice through a cone. It can't be drawn with a compass because of its continuously changing radii, but it can be constructed using a precise mathematical formula. However, you can eschew the math and draw an ellipse using a pencil, a string, and two pins, as explained in detail on p. 159. Alternatively, you can use a machine like the one shown in the photo at right.

An oval can be any form considered to be egg shaped, although it can also be symmetrical. A symmetrical oval can be drawn with a compass because it consists of two pairs of arcs, with one pair having a smaller radius than the other. The only information you need to construct it is the height and width of the desired oval.

▶ See *"Creating a Symmetrical Oval"* on p. 160.

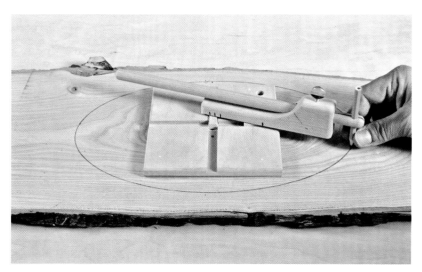

Setup for Sawing Curves

Sawing curves is the bandsaw's stock in trade. The tool's ability to run a narrow blade allows sawing curves of virtually any diameter, from a ⅛-in. radius on up. And the variety of available blades makes it easy to customize the saw setup for curves of specific radii. That said, it can't do the job well unless you're using the proper blade and guide setup.

This trammel of Archimedes made by Ovalgraph can quickly scribe accurate ellipse patterns.

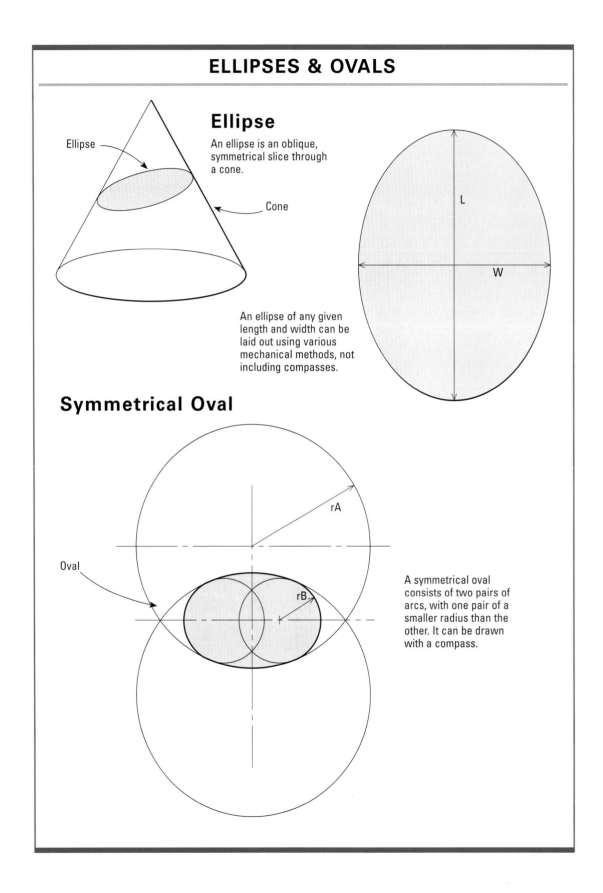

ELLIPSES & OVALS

Ellipse

Ellipse

An ellipse is an oblique, symmetrical slice through a cone.

Cone

An ellipse of any given length and width can be laid out using various mechanical methods, not including compasses.

L

W

Symmetrical Oval

rA

Oval

rB

A symmetrical oval consists of two pairs of arcs, with one pair of a smaller radius than the other. It can be drawn with a compass.

Proper Blade

When setting up a bandsaw for curve-cutting, the first consideration is selecting a blade with the proper width and tooth type. Blades narrower than ½ in. are best suited to sawing long, sweeping curves. The tighter the radius, the narrower the blade required. For tighter curves, you'll want to use a blade ¼ in. or narrower. Complete information on choosing blades is available in Section 3, but I'll recap here the fundamentals on blades used for curves.

[TIP] Always use a sharp blade, and let the blade do the work. Forcing it in the cut will result in a rough-cut face and wandering cut line.

Start by determining the tightest radius to be sawn. (See the chart on p. 63.) A blade that is too wide for a tight radius will bind,

> See *"Maximum Blade Widths for Curve Cuts"* on p. 63.

burn, and possibly even break. It may get bound up far enough into the cut that you can't easily back it out of the cut. In that case, shut the saw off and wiggle and jiggle the blade out of the kerf, trying not to pull it out of the guides. But it's best to avoid the problem altogether by simply outfitting the saw with the correct blade to begin with.

Cutting curves in wood creates a combination of stringy fibers (from ripping) and short, densely packed fibers (from crosscutting) that must be evacuated from the saw cut via the blade gullets. Big gullets—found on lower-pitch blades (with fewer teeth per inch)—transport the sawdust most effectively. However, a low-pitch blade leaves a

rough-cut face that will need to be smoothed by pattern routing, drum sanding, hand planing, or other processes more aggressive than hand sanding. High-pitch hook-tooth blades will cut smoother and provide better cutting control but will still require some work to clean up the saw marks.

Regular-tooth blades, with their 0° hook angle, offer a smoother, less aggressive cutting action than hook-tooth blades, but their smaller gullets require slower feed rates. The small gullets also tend to get gummed up when cutting resinous woods. Regular-tooth blades are best suited for sawing thin stock, where a high tooth count is essential.

Skip-tooth blades, which have 0° hook angles and large gullets, cut fairly cleanly but at the cost of some cutting vibration. The cut is rougher than that from a regular-tooth blade, and the skip teeth don't cut as quickly as hook teeth.

My choice for a good general curve-cutting blade is a ¼-in. 6-tpi hook-tooth blade. For tight-radius cuts, a ⅛-in. 14-tpi blade will handle the curves, although it's slow going in thick stock. If long, sweeping

A blade that is too wide for the radius being sawn will bind and burn the workpiece.

TIGHT, SMOOTH CURVES

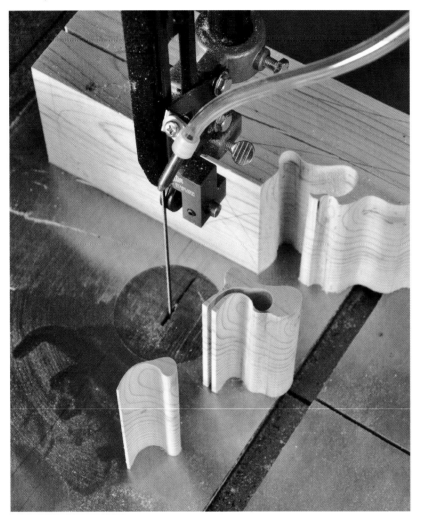

A ⅛-in. 14-tpi regular-tooth blade can make very tight-radius cuts in thick stock. The regular-tooth shape leaves a very clean cut that requires minimal smoothing.

Guides

Proper blade operation depends on accurately set blade guides, as discussed at length in Section 2. When sawing curves, the adjustment of the side guides is particularly important because they prevent the blade from twisting in operation, allowing the controlled cutting of an accurately steered workpiece. Because side guides provide resistance to the twisting forces involved in curved cutting, they should be positioned immediately behind the blade gullets to provide maximum support across the body of the blade.

Adjusting the guide assembly to within ¼ in. of the surface of the workpiece is critically important when cutting curves. If the guides are too far above the work, the unsupported section of blade can twist more easily, resulting in a wandering cut.

curves are the order of the day, a ½-in. 6-tpi blade will do the job nicely. The additional width helps the blade track to the cut line. For thin stock, remember that there should be about three teeth passing through the wood. So for ½-in.-thick stock, use a 6-tpi blade. For ¼-in.-thick stock, work with at least 12 teeth per inch.

[TIP] **Sawing resinous woods such as pine requires a blade with large gullets to effectively evacuate sawdust from the cut. Low-pitch hook-tooth blades are best.**

Position the side guides directly behind the blade gullets for maximum support of the blade body.

Of the various types of blade guides, I prefer block guides when it comes to curved cutting because they can be adjusted directly against the sides of the blade for the best support. Accurately set roller guides can also do a satisfactory job, although the rounded shoulder of the bearing can result in compromised support of narrow blades. This is particularly a problem with $\frac{3}{16}$-in. and $\frac{1}{8}$-in. blades. By eliminating play between the side guides and the blade, you gain very accurate control over blade twist for curved cutting.

Guiding Narrow Blades

Guiding narrow blades can be problematic, particularly if your saw is equipped with side rollers. As an alternative to using side rollers, Carter Products and Powermatic offer special thrust bearings that include a groove in the edge of a roller bearing to support and guide narrow blades without the need for side guides. If your saw is equipped with phenolic, plastic, or wood side guides, you

Blade guides set too far above the workpiece will allow the blade to twist, making it difficult to follow a cut line accurately.

Powermatic's grooved thrust bearing provides both thrust and side support for narrow blades such as this $\frac{3}{16}$-in. 18-tpi regular-tooth blade.

can adjust the guides directly against the sides of the blade, but you'll still need to provide rear support from the thrust bearing.

Basic Sawing Procedures

Cutting curves requires more concentration than rip cutting. With the correct blade installed and the guides accurately adjusted, you can easily and smoothly cut curves as long as you follow the basic procedures that I discuss here. But first, let me point out that two of the most important lessons to learn when cutting curves are patience and practice. Taking it slow and practicing on scrap will help improve your skills enormously. As you're learning, I recommend warming up by sawing a series of diminishing radius curves laid out with a French curve. Work with a variety of scrap stock, including thick and thin hardwood and softwood.

[TIP] **To accurately saw to a line, you have to be able to see it clearly. Always light your work area well.**

Leave a Little

Sawing tight to a cut line is a skill that takes practice to consistently achieve good results. Ideally, you want the sawn edge to require no more than a bit of hand sanding to clean up any residual saw marks. Realistically, though, you'll probably have to smooth the cuts by machine-sanding to the cut line or perhaps by pattern-routing to the final shape. Because of that, it's a good idea to saw slightly outside your cut line. Of course, the closer you saw to the line without hiccups, especially on tight inside radius curves, the less cleanup you'll have to do. I try to veer

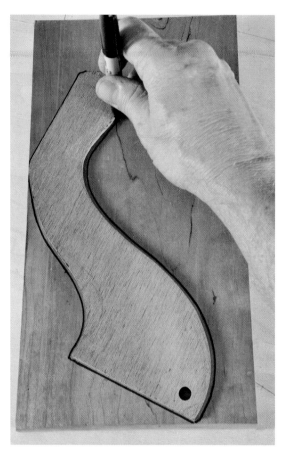

When laying out a bandsaw cut line using a router template, slightly offset the cut line from the template edge. After sawing, the workpiece will be routed to final shape by guiding a flush-trim bit against the template.

no farther than about $\frac{1}{32}$ in. from the line. This is where practice yields big benefits.

When I plan on pattern-routing bandsawn parts to final shape, I use the router template to lay out the saw cut lines. By tracing around the perimeter with a fine felt-tipped marker held vertically, a slight offset is created. After sawing to this line, I rout the edge of the workpiece to final size using the template and a flush-trim bit.

Stay ahead of the Curve

While sawing curves, many beginners make the mistake of focusing on the spot where the saw teeth enter the surface of the workpiece. Unfortunately, this leads to overcorrection as unanticipated changes in the cut line suddenly appear. You can avoid unpleasant surprises by mentally practicing the cut first. Before turning on the saw, scrutinize the curves, paying particular attention to potential trouble spots such as very tight sections. Also make sure that you'll have enough room to swing the workpiece without smacking into the saw frame.

> [TIP] Always warm up to sawing your project parts by making a few representative curved cuts in scrap of similar thickness and species.

Feed Straight On to the Blade

Learn to steer the workpiece so that the cut line approaches the blade straight on. The idea is to avoid putting side pressure against the blade, which will cause it to twist, wander, and possibly break. (As explained earlier, properly adjusted blade guides will also help prevent blade twist.) When sawing, concentrate on pushing straight on into the blade while keeping your hands where they can maneuver the workpiece without constant repositioning.

Sawing Simple Curves

Gentle curves are easy to cut. Simply follow a line scribed on the workpiece or drawn on an affixed pattern. Make sure to feed straight on into the blade, avoiding sideways pressure. Gradual curves should be sawn as quickly as the blade allows, as long as

► BACK UP WITH CAUTION

Try to avoid backing the blade out of a cut. Short, straight cuts are relatively safe to exit from backward, but add even a slight amount of curve to the cut and you run the risk of binding the blade in the kerf and possibly pulling the blade off the wheels. If the blade gets pinched in a long, curved cut that requires backing out of, you can insert a small wedge at the entry point to help relieve pressure on the blade for easier removal. Always turn the saw off before backing out of a curved cut of any sort.

you're able to follow the cut line. Too slow a feed speed denies the blade bite, causing it to hunt a bit, which can result in a wobbling cut.

Sawing Circles

Sawing accurate circles is best done with a jig like the one shown on p. 155. However, it can be done freehand in a pinch, although it's challenging. To help with the job, I boldly mark the center of the circle on the workpiece blank, and then add a diameter line. Using the line as a reference, I locate

► See *"A Basic Circle-Cutting Jig"* on p. 155.

▶ ORCHESTRATING A COMPLEX CURVE

Sawing complex curves requires a plan of action to ensure efficient, clean cutting. Avoid trouble by following these three guidelines: Proceed in an orderly fashion; don't trap the blade at the end of a curved cut; and make long, sweeping cuts to produce the fairest curves. For example, here's one approach for cutting a corbel with a complex curve:

- Cut #1: Saw the bottom cove in one sweeping cut.

- Cut #2: Make a relief cut to free the large offcut created by #3.

- Cut #3: The entire cut made in one smooth pass ensures a fair curve.

- Cut #4: Same as #1, a single cut creates a fair cove.

- Cuts #5 & #6: Relief cuts for the subsequent sharp curve cuts #7 & #8.

- Cut #7: Entering from the top, cut to apex of arc, following around to relief cut.

- Cut #8: From arc apex, follow the curve to the relief cut.

- Cuts #9 & #10: Mating cuts create the notch.

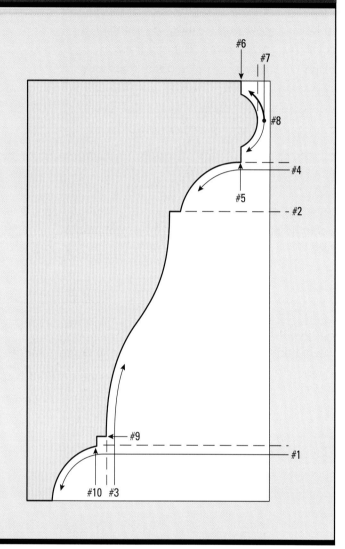

To saw a circle freehand, mark a diameter line running through its center point, position the circle center in line with the blade teeth, and rotate the workpiece to make the cut.

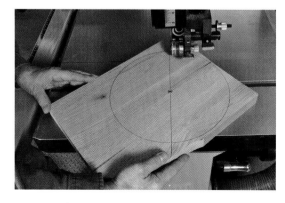

the center point of the circle directly in line with the leading edge of the blade, precisely as a circle-cutting guide would hold it. To make the cut, I envision pivoting around that imaginary center point while trying to avoid any side pressure on the blade. The process is as tricky as it sounds, but here again, practice can make the task become routine.

Tight Scroll Cutting

Tight scroll cutting, especially in thick material, can be challenging. However, by following a few simple rules, your success is virtually guaranteed. First of all, use a blade as narrow as ⅛ in., and make sure your guides are adjusted properly. You'll have to feed the work fairly slowly due to the small tooth gullets, but don't go so slowly that heat builds up in the saw cut. Try to keep moving at a steady pace and avoid placing any side pressure against the blade. When sawing resinous woods such as pine, use a brass kitchen brush as frequently as necessary to clean the blade gullets of pitch.

Smoothing Curved Work

Even the best bandsaw blades, the most scrupulously set-up saw, and the most careful sawing procedures will still leave saw marks on the freshly cut face. There are many methods of removing the saw marks, including planing, scraping, and sanding. Each technique has its benefits and drawbacks. Understanding them will help you develop a specific plan for cleaning up your curves.

Hand Sanding

Hand sanding is a good way to eliminate saw marks on curved cuts. Like any sanding procedure, it's very important to move in sequence through the appropriate sandpaper grits. Don't just jump from coarse to fine in an effort to save time. Very fine sandpaper will not remove the scratches from coarse paper. You need to move through the intermediate grits. I typically start with 80-grit paper to quickly remove the saw marks, and then proceed progressively through 100-,

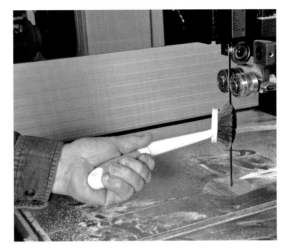

Tight scroll cutting requires the use of narrow, fine-pitch regular-tooth blades that can quickly clog with sawdust. A brass brush works great for cleaning the gullets.

> ## THE ORIGINS OF SCROLLWORK

"Scroll cuts" are tight curved cuts typically used to embellish furniture or millwork. The word *scrollsawing* is derived from the ancient term for a roll of paper—particularly parchment—called a scroll. The gradually diminishing circles seen at the end of the paper rolls inspired the use of scrolls as design elements in everything from violin heads to the volutes in Ionic and Corinthian capitals. The eventual appearance of tightly cut decorative circles cut into woodwork came to be called scrollwork.

Sanding blocks can be made in virtually any size or shape to suit a given curve or contour. Spray adhesive can be used to hold the sandpaper onto the block.

These shopmade sandpaper files are simply thin sticks of wood with sandpaper glued to them. The stepped shape allows access to ever-tighter quarters.

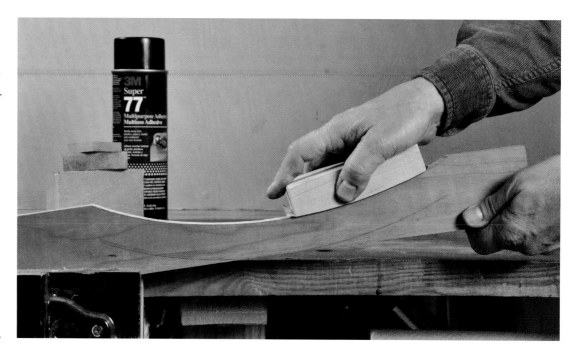

120-, 150-, and 180-, typically ending with 220-grit.

Use sanding blocks. Working with only your hand as a sandpaper backer tends to round over crisp, square edges. I make my sanding blocks from scrapwood in a variety of sizes. I glue the sandpaper on using 3M's No. 77 spray adhesive, which allows easy replacement of worn paper. To help maintain a fair curve, a sanding block can be shaped to the same radius as any long curved piece.

Smoothing interior surfaces of scroll cuts and other tight curves requires special tools. Emery fingernail files work fine for removing light saw marks, but they aren't available in very coarse grits for heavier work. A better solution is to make narrow sandpaper "files" from thin wood scraps with the paper glued to them. I make my files in stepped form, providing versatility for working in a variety of tight situations.

Hand-Tooling

Removing saw marks with hand tools is both quick and efficient. Curved edges typically consist of both face grain and end grain, so blades must be kept sharp and accurately adjusted to avoid chatter marks or tearout. Cutting with the slope of the grain is paramount for getting good results. Therefore, a few minutes spent analyzing the piece and sketching a few directional marks can save time and grief in the long run. Again, practice is the key. Spend some time working with a few curved scraps to learn how best to approach the curves.

Card Scraper

A card scraper is a thin, flexible piece of steel with a cutting burr burnished onto the long edges. Handled with skill, a properly sharpened and burnished scraper is capable of removing saw marks quickly and leaving a finish-ready surface. In fact, a scraper will more quickly do a much better job than sandpaper when it comes to smoothing the faces of parts such as serpentine drawer fronts or curved table aprons.

A properly sharpened card scraper will remove saw marks much more efficiently than sandpaper.

SHOPMADE SANDING FILES

¾ in.

¼ in.

8 in.

5 in.

¼ in.

2½ in.

¼ in.

Make several files by cutting steps in ¾-in. x 2-in. x 8-in. pine, then rip into ⅛-in. strips.

Spray adhesive on a sheet of sandpaper, apply wood strips, and cut out the profile with a hobby knife.

The only drawback to using a card scraper on curved forms is that the scraper needs to be oriented slightly diagonal to the saw marks to avoid creating a rippled surface. Therefore, scraping a narrow edge on a concave curve might present a challenge.

Spokeshave

A spokeshave is basically a short-soled plane with handles on either side of the blade. Originally designed for shaping round wheel spokes, a sharp, well-adjusted spokeshave can quickly cut a thin shaving off the edge of a board to clean up bandsaw marks.

Spokeshaves are available with flat or curved bottoms. Flat-bottom spokeshaves work best on flat surfaces or convex curves. A round-bottom spokeshave, with its curved sole, works well for removing bandsaw marks on concave curves. Round-bottom spokeshaves are available commercially, but I converted my Stanley No. 53 adjustable-throat spokeshave from a flat to a curved bottom by rounding the sole to a 5-in. radius. The adjustable throat allows finer shaving control than the open throat on a typical curved-bottom model.

Compass Plane

The *compass*, or *circular*, plane combines a thin, flexible spring-steel sole with an adjustment system that secures the sole at a deter-

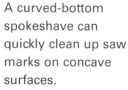

A curved-bottom spokeshave can quickly clean up saw marks on concave surfaces.

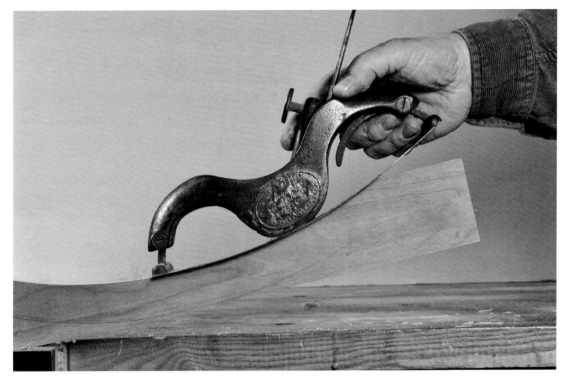

This 1860s compass plane has a flexible sole that can be set to the radius of a curve, much like its modern counterparts.

mined radius. This allows the tool to plane a precise radius on convex or concave shapes. As when using any handplane, pay attention to the wood's grain direction to avoid tearout, as shown in the drawing at right.

Drum Sanders

Power sanding is a quick way to remove saw marks, particularly on long, sweeping curves. Small sanding drums can be purchased economically for mounting in a power drill or drill press. This minimal approach works fine in some cases, but it's asking a lot from a small drum. And in the case of a drill press, the machine's column can impede full 360° access to the work.

A much better approach is an oscillating spindle sander. These machines consist of a vertical spindle-mounted drum that projects up through a table that supports the work being sanded. Drums of various diameters

USING A COMPASS PLANE

To avoid tearout, plane with the slope of the grain.

Convex curve
Work from the middle of the curve toward the ends.

Concave curve
Start at the ends and work downhill toward the middle.

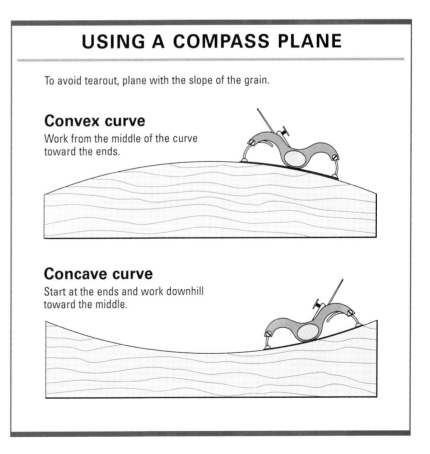

A spindle sander can be outfitted with sanding drums of different diameters for easy smoothing of just about any curve.

Belt & Disk Sanders

Belt and disk sanders are of some use in smoothing curves, although their flat platens tend to limit them primarily to sanding convex forms. On some stationary belt sanders, the nose guard can be removed to allow access to the wheel for sanding concave curves. However, this can be clumsy if there's no table to support the workpiece for the operation.

When sanding convex curves against a disk or flat-belt sander platen, only a tiny section of the workpiece is actually contacting the disk or belt, which can make sanding fair curves difficult. Try to use long, sweeping strokes to help mitigate a lumpy edge.

With a little creativity, a portable belt sander can be converted into a stationary edge sander. It's not hard to design a custom jig for your particular sander that will hold it on its side while providing a support for the workpiece. You can even slip a curved wooden block under the platen to allow sanding of slight concave curves.

Template Routing

Template routing is a very useful way to clean up bandsawn edges while creating very accurate duplicate parts. After bandsawing the workpiece slightly outside the cut lines, attach a template to it using double-face tape, hot melt glue, or brads. Then rout against the edge of the template using a flush-trim bit to duplicate the template shape.

The biggest drawback to routing curved edges is that the bit is often cutting against the slope of the grain instead of with it, which can cause tearout. The solution is to *climb-cut* those areas, moving the router in

can be used to accommodate different curves and will accept sleeves of various grits. On an oscillating spindle sander, the drum moves up and down as it rotates, minimizing sanding scratches and sawdust overload on the drum.

A big benefit of spindle sanders is the easy access to all sides of the drum, which allows for making long, sweeping sanding strokes that contribute to fair curves. Short, slow strokes will leave divots and other irregularities. Light pressure is best. As with any sanding procedure, follow the grits in sequence from coarse to fine. Skipping grits ultimately costs more time to sand the edge smooth. It also prematurely wears out the finer-grit drums, which gets expensive.

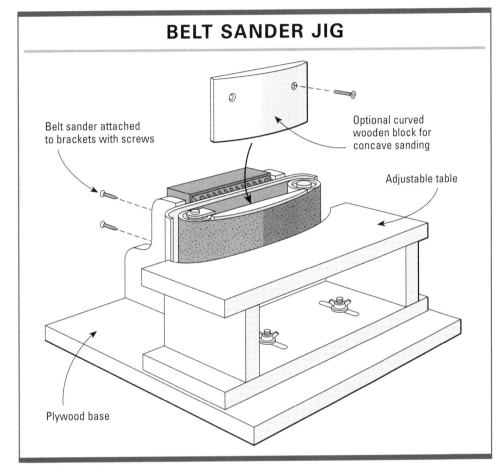

BELT SANDER JIG

Belt sander attached to brackets with screws

Optional curved wooden block for concave sanding

Adjustable table

Plywood base

Before affixing a router template to a workpiece for edge trimming, indicate on the template the direction of router travel that will minimize grain tearout.

a clockwise direction instead of the normal counterclockwise motion around a workpiece. Care has to be taken when climb-cutting to avoid kickback and loss of control of the router. Move slowly while holding the tool firmly against the template. Finish up by completely routing around the workpiece in a counterclockwise direction, which will pull the router tightly against the template to remove any residual bumps or blips.

When the template is fastened to the workpiece, you won't be able to see the wood grain direction. Therefore, analyze the grain directions and make notations on the template to indicate the desired direction of cut before you attach it to the workpiece.

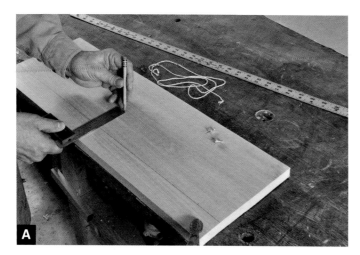

A

B

C

Arc Layout with String

Arcs can be drawn with nothing more than a string, a pencil, and a couple of nails. Start by laying out the baseline (arc chord) and the arc height at the center of the chord **(A)**. Drive a small brad into the stock at each end of the base-line, leaving the nail mostly proud. (Map pins will work with softer wood.) Using a length of string that is more than double the baseline length, wrap it around the nails and knot it together to create a continuous-loop triangle that just reaches the top of the arc without stretching easily beyond it **(B)**. Use string that has minimal stretch. Cotton packaging string will work, but be careful when scribing the arc not to put too much pressure against the string or the curve won't end up fair.

Place a soft lead pencil inside the string at the arc height line, forming a triangle with the string. While pinching the pencil to the string at one point, use your other hand to help pull the string around the pins, keeping steady pressure against the string with your pencil hand. Drag the string and pencil to one end, and then return to the middle and repeat the procedure, moving to the other end. This method requires careful coordina-tion of string pressure and string feed to get a smooth arc **(C)**.

Arc Layout
Using a Flexible Strip

One of the simplest ways to lay out an arc is to flex a thin strip of wood between two fixed points. The flexible strip can be made of hardboard or any straight-grained wood. Just make sure the strip is of a constant width and thickness throughout its length. Otherwise, differences in density may not allow it to bend uniformly. I typically make my strips 1/8 in. x 3/4 in. wide and a few inches longer than the arc baseline. If the arc is larger than about 36 in. between the fixed points, I make the strip a bit thicker to create more resistance during the bend, resulting in a smoother arc.

To lay out the arc, begin by marking out its baseline. Next, mark the height of the arc at the center of the baseline **(A)**. In this case, I'm using the edge of the board as the arc baseline, so there's no room to drive nails for strip restraints. Instead, I'm clamping pads to the board. This avoids nail holes while providing good support points for the wood strip to flex against **(B)**. Place the flex strip against the two pads and bend it until its edge meets the registration mark. Keep the pivot points and height mark on the same side of the flexible strip, and carefully trace the arc with a soft lead pencil **(C)**. Take care to not exert pressure against the strip with the pencil while tracing the arc, as it's easy to distort the flexible strip from a fair curve.

[TIP] If nails are used as restraints for creating an arc, snip their heads off after driving them partially in, providing a straight, smooth surface for the flex strip to slide against.

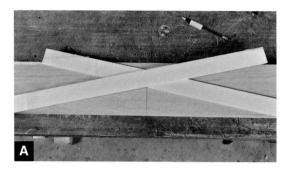

A

B

C

D

E

Two-Board Arc Layout

Drawing an arc with a very large radius using string, a flexible strip, or a long beam compass can be cumbersome. It's difficult to keep the string uniformly taut over a long distance, long flexible strips can flex erratically, and a long beam compass requires a large space in which to work. A good alternative in these cases is to use two boards fastened together at an angle derived from the base chord and the height of the arc. To scribe the arc, you simply slide the attached boards over two fixed pivot points.

Make the assembly using two sticks, each of which is about a foot longer than the baseline of the desired arc. Then lay out the baseline and the height of the arc. Place the sticks so that they touch the ends of the baseline while intersecting precisely with the end of the arc height layout line **(A)**. Secure the sticks together at that angle using tacks, hot-melt glue, or double-face tape **(B)**.

Now clamp a couple of pivot blocks in place, aligning them with the outside edge of the workpiece at the ends of the arc chord **(C)**. To draw the arc, place the tip of a pencil at the intersection of the sticks and carefully slide the sticks across the pivot points **(D)**. I usually scribe one side of the arc at a time, working from the center down to each end to create the arc **(E)**.

Making a Beam Compass

A handy beam compass can be fabricated from a ³⁄₈-in.-dia. dowel, a couple blocks of wood, a pencil, and a wood screw **(A)**. The blocks act as trammel heads, with the headstock holding a pencil and the pivot block holding a screw that serves as a pivot point. A saw kerf cut partway through the head block turns it into a sort of spring clamp for holding the pencil. A partial kerf in the pivot block allows clamping it to the rod after adjusting its position relative to the headstock.

Make each block 1¹⁄₂ in. square x 3 in. long, and then drill the holes in the headstock as shown in the drawing **(B)**. The ¹⁄₄-in.-dia. hole is for the pencil, the ³⁄₈-in.-dia. hole is to accept the rod, and the ¹⁄₈-in.-dia. hole reduces the chance of the block splitting in use. Bandsaw a kerf through the ¹⁄₄-in. hole and into the ¹⁄₈-in. hole **(C)**, and then glue the headstock to the end of a ³⁄₈-in.-dia. dowel whose length serves your needs. To install or reposition a pencil in the block, insert a screwdriver in the saw kerf and twist it just enough to relieve the clamping pressure on the pencil **(D)**.

Next, drill the ³⁄₈-in.-dia. and ¹⁄₈-in.-dia. holes through the pivot block as shown in the drawing. **(E)**. Also bandsaw a kerf through the larger hole and into the smaller. Rebore the upper half of the ¹⁄₈-in.-dia. hole to create a slip-fit "clearance hole" for a #10 x 1³⁄₄-in. wood screw. This screw serves as both the pivot point and also as a means of clamping the pivot block to the dowel at the desired location. Before installing the screw, I grind away the last few threads, which eases positioning of the point in use **(F)**. Slip the pivot block onto the dowel, position it as desired, and tighten the screw to lock the pivot block in place **(G)**.

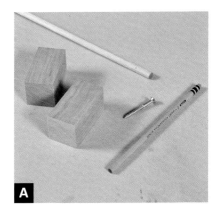

A

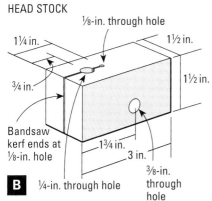

HEAD STOCK

¹⁄₈-in. through hole

1¹⁄₄ in.   1¹⁄₂ in.

¾ in.   1¹⁄₂ in.

Bandsaw kerf ends at ¹⁄₈-in. hole

1³⁄₄ in.   3 in.

³⁄₈-in. through hole

B   ¹⁄₄-in. through hole

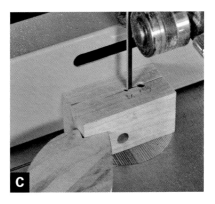

C

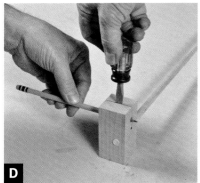

D

PIVOT BLOCK

¹⁄₈-in. through hole

¾ in.   3 in.

Section above saw kerf rebored for slip-fit of #10 1³⁄₄-in. wood screw

1¹⁄₂ in.   ¾ in.

½ in.

1³⁄₄ in.   2¹⁄₄ in.

1¹⁄₂ in.

¹⁄₈-in. through hole

Bandsaw kerf ends at ¹⁄₈-in. hole.

³⁄₈-in. through hole

E

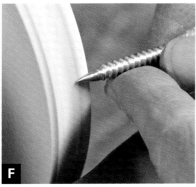

F

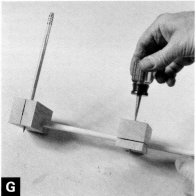

G

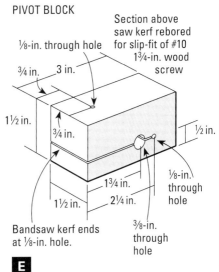

Using a Beam Compass

To lay out a large arc using a beam compass, begin by clamping the workpiece across one end of your bench. Then take a strip of material the same thickness as your workpiece and at least as long as the radius of your desired arc, and place the strip perpendicular to your workpiece at its center **(A)**. This places the trammel points on the same plane, which makes scribing the arc easier.

Measure and mark the height of the arc above its chord, and then lock the trammel points to the beam, separating them by a distance equal to the arc's radius **(B)**. Push the point securely into the wood at the centerline and position the pencil at the height of the arc **(C)**. Now carefully pull the pencil through its arc **(D)**.

A Basic Circle-Cutting Jig

A simple circle-cutting jig can be made from a piece of plywood and a scrapwood block. In use, the plywood serves as a carrier board with a pivot point around which the workpiece blank rotates. The scrapwood block simply acts as a set-up stop.

Begin by sizing the plywood carrier board. Make it the full depth of the saw table from front to back. To determine the width, add at least several inches to the radius of the desired circle. The wider the better, because the more support under the workpiece, the easier it will be to control.

Next, lock the saw's rip fence in place a couple of inches to the left of the blade, and securely clamp the scrap wood block to the back edge of the table or onto the rear rip fence rail **(A)**. Holding the plywood carrier board tight to the rip fence, saw into the board until the plywood stops against the block **(B)**.

Remove the plywood, flip it over, and draw a line perpendicular to the kerf, beginning at its end **(C)**. Make sure the line extending from the kerf is at least as long as your intended radius. Measure over from the kerf a distance equal to the radius, and mark your pivot point **(D)**. Then drive a short nail completely into the board at that location **(E)**. Flip the plywood back over and clip the nail, leaving a projection of about ⅛ in **(F)**. The jig is now ready to use, as shown in the following photo essay.

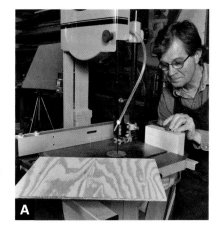

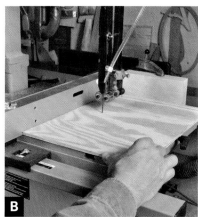

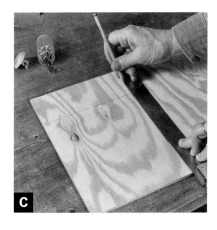

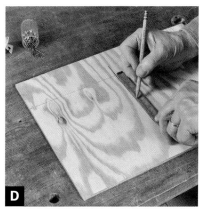

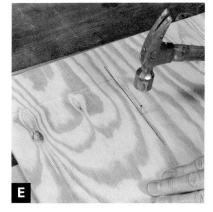

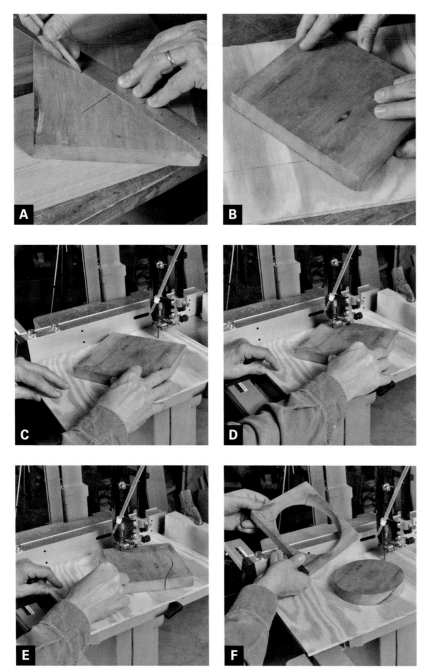

Using a Basic Circle-Cutting Jig

It's easy to use the basic circle-cutting jig shown in the previous photo essay. Start by marking out the center of the stock to be sawn **(A)**. Drill or punch a small, shallow hole at that location that's just large enough to accommodate the nail pivot point on the plywood carrier board. With the carrier board removed from the bandsaw, place the stock onto the pivot point and rotate the stock to make sure its corners will clear the saw fence when the carrier board is in place **(B)**. If they don't, simply rough-saw enough of the corners off to provide the necessary clearance.

Place the workpiece-mounted carrier board tight to the bandsaw fence, and then feed it forward into the blade while holding the workpiece to prevent it from spinning **(C)**. Continue sawing until the carrier board contacts the stop at the rear of the saw **(D)**. At this point, begin rotating the stock around the pivot point to saw the circle **(E)**. When the cut is finished, turn off the saw and allow it to stop before you remove the workpiece. You should now have a perfect circle **(F)**.

Making a Curve Template

Templates are hard copies of initial paper patterns and an ideal way to transfer a pattern to a workpiece. A template will survive multiple uses, whereas a pattern is often used as a consumable cutting guide that is glued directly to the workpiece. Templates can be made from hardboard, medium-density fiberboard (MDF), Baltic birch plywood, or acrylic.

You make a curved template in much the same way you would make a part from a pattern. Attach a sacrificial copy of your pattern to your template material using nonpermanent adhesive for easy removal afterward **(A)**. Saw the shape, staying $1/32$ in. or so outside the pattern lines **(B)**. Afterward, carefully sand, plane, or file exactly to the line, making sure the edge is smooth and fair. Care taken with this step is time well spent, as the edge will be the guide surface for trimming your final project parts **(C)**.

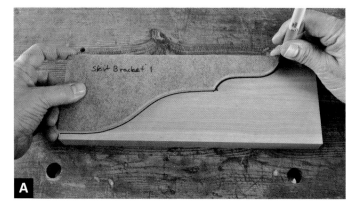

Using a Curve Template

To employ a curve template most efficiently, first use it to trace the shape onto the project part **(A)**. Then bandsaw the waste to within ⅟₁₆ in. or so of the actual pattern line **(B)**.

When you're done, mount the pattern to the workpiece within the original layout lines. You can use small brads or screws if you're attaching it to the underside or backside of a piece that won't show in the finished project. Otherwise, use double-face tape, which won't damage the work **(C)**. Before applying tape, make sure the contacting surfaces are free of dust, and apply enough pressure to ensure that the template won't slip. Using a lot of tape is a safe bet, but this can make the template difficult to remove afterward. If you use a few small pieces of tape, you can clamp the parts together for a few moments to ensure good contact.

Finish up by routing the edges with a flush-trim bit whose bearing follows the edges of the template **(D)**. In the photo, I'm doing the trimming on a router table, with the template facing downward. The auxiliary guide pin on the table provides leverage and additional support for the workpiece, greatly aiding feed control.

String Layout for Ellipse

Laying out an ellipse is fairly easy. All you need is a pencil, two pins, a piece of string, and a compass. Start by determining the rectangle that describes the height and width of your desired ellipse. Draw a cross, with the horizontal line (AB) representing the width of the ellipse and the vertical line (CD) representing the height **(A)**. Next, set a compass to half the length of line AB. Place one end of the compass at point D, and swing the compass to locate points X and Y (the foci) on line AB **(B)**. Then insert push pins at those foci points. Tie a piece of non-stretching string (I prefer waxed muslin) in a loop that reaches points X, Y, and C **(C)**. Stretch the line taut with a pencil held vertically, and carefully scribe the ellipse **(D)**.

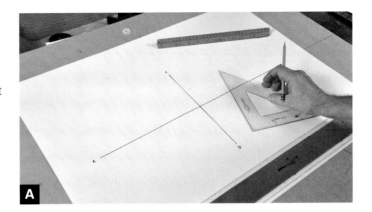

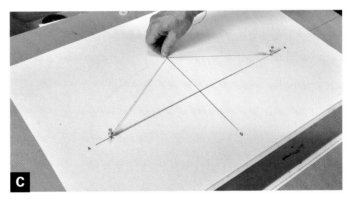

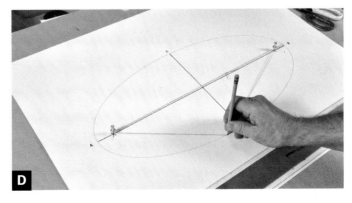

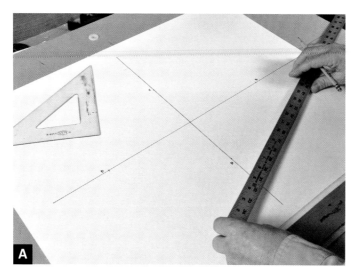

A

B

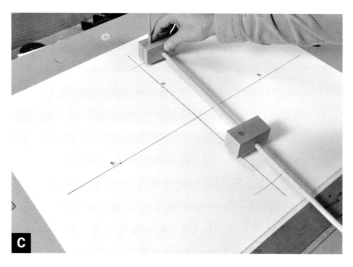

C

Creating a Symmetrical Oval

The shape of a symmetrical oval can be very useful in woodworking project design. Although similar to an ellipse, it is actually a different geometrical construct. A symmetrical oval is created from two intersecting circles with differing radii. Therefore, it can be quickly constructed using a compass, a ruler, and a mathematical formula.

As an example, let's construct an oval here that's 15 in. long x 9 in. wide. Start by laying out a horizontal and a vertical axis that intersect at their midpoints. On the horizontal axis, mark points A and B to define the oval's 15-in. length. On the vertical axis, mark C and D to define its 9-in. width **(A)**. Now we'll use the following formula to determine the radii of the arcs for constructing a symmetrical oval:

$(8AB - 5CD) \div 6 = $ long radius

$(4CD - AB) \div 6 = $ short radius

So, for our oval, the radius of the long arc works out like this:

$(8 \times 15 - 5 \times 9) \div 6$

$(120 - 45) \div 6$

$75 \div 6 = $ **12.5 in.**

And for the radius of the short arc:

$(4 \times 9 - 15) \div 6$

$(36 - 15) \div 6$

$21 \div 6 = $ **3.5 in.**

Set your compass to 12½ in. **(B)**. Locate the compass pivot at point D, and scribe a line through the lower section of the vertical axis. Then repeat the process, this time locating the compass pivot at point C and swinging through the upper section of the vertical axis **(C)**.

Now place the compass pivot at the upper intersection you just created, and swing an arc through C. Repeat the process, pivoting from the lower intersection and swinging through point D **(D)**.

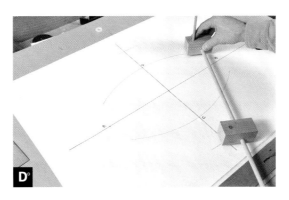

Next, set a compass to 3½ in. to define the radius of the short arc **(E)**. Pivoting the compass from point B, scribe a line across the horizontal axis **(F)**. Now pivot the compass from the intersection you just scribed to create the arc that completes one end of the oval **(G)**. Repeat the process at point A to close the oval.

The two sets of arcs should blend nearly imperceptibly. If the sections where they meet aren't quite fair, a French curve can quickly smooth things out **(H)**.

Advanced Cutting Techniques

Compound Sawing

➤ Basic Cut-and-Tape Compound Sawing (p. 172)

➤ "Four-Square" Compound Sawing (p. 173)

Curved Moldings

➤ Curved Cock Beading (p. 174)

➤ Curved Built-Up Moldings (p. 176)

Making Tenons

➤ Sawing Round Tenons (p. 177)

➤ Tenon Shoulder Jig (p. 178)

➤ Sawing Tenon Cheeks (p. 180)

➤ Bridle Joint (p. 181)

➤ Basic Stack Sawing (p. 183)

Special Techniques

➤ Decorative Stack Sawing (p. 184)

➤ Bandsaw Boxes (p. 185)

➤ Featherboard Cutting Jig (p. 187)

➤ Making a Featherboard (p. 189)

➤ Pattern Sawing (p. 190)

Slabbing Logs

➤ Log Sawing Sled (p. 191)

➤ Using a Log Sawing Sled (p. 194)

I N THE PRECEDING SECTIONS, I discussed how to set up a bandsaw, how to choose the proper blade, and how to rip, resaw, and cut basic curves. Now let's take that accumulated knowledge and push the envelope a bit. In this section, I'll show you methods for making compound cuts that will reveal a whole new world of design possibilities. You'll also learn how to build and use a variety of jigs for making featherboards and slabbing logs. To top it off, I'll introduce you to a host of quick, easy techniques that will help you have fun building your furniture and other projects.

Sawing Compound Curves

Cutting compound curves usually involves sawing multiple profiles on a workpiece. The typical maneuver is the same one used for cutting a shapely cabriole leg, where a profile is sawn through one face of the stock before rotating the piece 90° to saw the other profile through the adjacent face. Sawing compound curves can produce spectacular results when properly executed, and the maneuver is a lot of fun to perform. There is a whole world of different shapes and combinations of cuts that can generate very creative results.

Cut-and-Tape Method

The cut-and-tape method is a very simple and effective approach for roughing out cabriole legs and other sculptural shapes. It also lends itself to experimenting with creative variations such as stacked sawing, as discussed later.

Here's the process in a nutshell: Make patterns of the front and side profiles and transfer the shapes to adjacent faces on the workpiece. You can either trace around the patterns or glue them directly to the stock. After sawing out one of the profiles, reattach the offcuts with tape to provide good cutting support and to reestablish your cut line for the second profile cut. After making the second cut, the roughed-out piece is ready for refinement with hand tools and sandpaper.

► See *"Basic Cut-and-Tape Compound Sawing"* on p. 172.

The "Four-Square" Method

There is a variation of the cut-and-tape method that I refer to as the "four-square" system, which uses the offcuts as part of the finished product. That is, after both profiles have been sawed into two parts, the four parts are then inverted and glued together.

► See *"'Four-Square' Compound Sawing"* on p. 173.

The technique allows making unusually shaped pieces that can be used for lamp stands, decorative posts, or very interesting furniture legs. As a side benefit, the method serves as a sort of "lumber stretcher," yielding parts with a finished outside dimension that exceeds the thickness of the original stock.

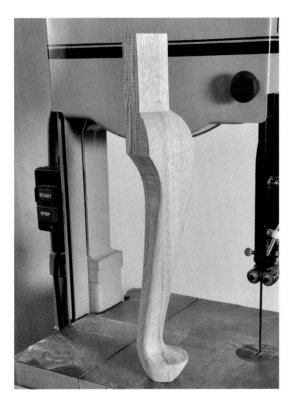

Curvaceous cabriole legs can be easily sawn on the bandsaw using the cut-and-tape method for sawing compound curves.

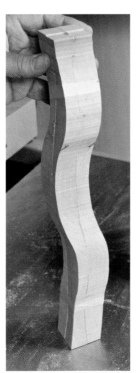

Interestingly shaped compound-curve parts can be easily created with the "four-square" sawing method. The technique, which involves regluing sawn parts back together, yields parts that exceed the thickness of the original stock.

Built-Up Curved Moldings

Intricate curved moldings can be created quite simply with the help of a bandsaw. For example, you can make a curved cock beading that adds elegance to doors, drawers, and crown molding or that simply serves as an embellishment on a long curved edge. Complex moldings with deep reveals and overhangs can also be shaped using basic router bits to mold the edges of multiple-part stacked assemblies. The technique allows you to build gooseneck moldings, among other exotic adornments.

Curved Cock Beading

A cock bead is typically a narrow bullnosed bead that surrounds a drawer front or door. However, it can also be used as an arched "eyebrow" molding or other form of decoration. Cock beads were commonly used on late 18th-century furniture to provide a shadow around doors and drawers to render the margins between the parts essentially invisible.

Straight cock beads are easily made by ripping narrow stock and shaping its edge with a router or scratch stock before fastening it to the edge of the board. Curved cock beading is a bit more difficult but well worth the effort. In fact, bandsawing the beading from the panel to which it's attached allows a perfect matchup of grain, color, and shape. The beauty of this method is that any slight deviation from the bandsawed cutline won't matter much because the error is mirrored between the two parts. When they are fastened back together, the error will be inconspicuous.

➤ See *"Curved Cock Beading"* on p. 174.

Curved Built-Up Moldings

Complex curved moldings can be constructed to create profiles that would be impossible to mold in one piece with a router or shaper. Lovely molding with deep reveals

Cock beading on this curved molding provides a nice shadow line at the top, enhancing the step-curved capital on this cupboard.

This two-part molding was sawn from a single piece separated into two. After the individual parts were shaped, they were rejoined, shifting one of the pieces inward to create a stepped design.

and large overhangs can be constructed by dividing the molding stock into strips of various widths, shaping the edges, ripping the strips to different widths, and reassembling them.

The gooseneck molding at the top of this cabinet was made by bandsawing the overall shape and then separating it into pieces that were individually shaped and then reglued together.

▶ See *"Curved Built-Up Moldings"* on p. 176.

Tenons

When it comes to cutting tenons, the bandsaw does a fine job. Multiple identical tenons can be sawed accurately by setting up the fence with stop blocks or by using simple jigs. The same sorts of setups allow you to make end rabbets and bridle joints. The latter is an "open" mortise-and-tenon joint that provides a very strong attachment for frame corners.

Whatever type of tenon or rabbet joint you're cutting, use a wide blade with at least 6 tpi, which will produce a smooth cut. My blade of choice for the job is generally a ½-in. 6-tpi hook-tooth blade.

(clockwise) End rabbets, bridle joints, and tenons are easily made on the bandsaw.

▶JOINERY ON THE BANDSAW

The bandsaw is an incredibly valuable tool for sawing circles and curves or for ripping and resawing timbers, but when it comes to cutting complex joinery such as dovetails, it falls short. I have tried many different methods and jigs that purport to create easy, tight dovetails or box joints and haven't found any that resulted in furniture-grade joinery without a lot of additional handwork. Most methods are overly complex or immensely time-consuming and don't yield good, repeatable results.

Yes, the bandsaw does a good job of making a variety of tenons and end rabbets on relatively narrow stock, but it can't be expected to make long-edge rabbets, cross laps, grooves, dadoes, or spline joints or perform other tasks best suited to a tablesaw or router. At best, it quickly removes waste material, leaving a square face that can then be pared or planed manually for a tight-fitting joint. For these reasons, you won't see instruction for dovetailing or other fussy joinery in this book. I simply believe there are better, more efficient ways of making tight-fitting joinery than with a bandsaw.

With a simple setup, the bandsaw can cut an accurately sized round tenon that is perfectly centered on the end of round stock.

Round Tenons

The bandsaw is a great tool for cutting round tenons on the ends of dowels and spindles. All that's required is a stop and a V-cradle. The cradle is clamped to the fence, with the bottom of the V offset the appropriate distance from the blade. A stop block clamped to the fence behind the blade determines the length of the tenon.

The tenon is cut by repeatedly advancing the dowel into the blade and "whittling" it down in a succession of cuts, rotating the stock between each cut. After the waste has been removed, a clean, square shoulder is created by simply turning the dowel counterclockwise in the cradle.

▶See *"Sawing Round Tenons"* on p. 177.

Sawing a Four-Shoulder Tenon

The most common type of tenon found in furniture is a four-shoulder tenon. When cutting this joint on the bandsaw, I find it makes the most sense to saw the shoulders of the joint first, then the cheeks.

Many woodworkers saw tenon cheeks on the bandsaw but leave the shoulder cutting to the tablesaw. That's because feeding workpieces with the bandsaw miter gauge requires great control to prevent cutting too deeply and possibly weakening the tenon in the process. To overcome this problem, I designed a jig that works along with the saw's miter gauge to accurately control cut depth and produce square, cleanly cut shoulders.

▶See *"Tenon Shoulder Jig"* on p. 178.

When sawing tenons, the flat stop block to the right arrests workpiece travel at the end of the cut. A previously sawn cheek sits in an "escape alley" between the stop block and fence.

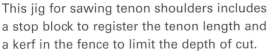

This jig for sawing tenon shoulders includes a stop block to register the tenon length and a kerf in the fence to limit the depth of cut.

Cutting tenon cheeks is easy, particularly if you use the simple setup described, which guarantees accurate stop cuts and precise dimensions. It's basically a simple matter

▶ See *"Sawing Tenon Cheeks"* on p. 180.

This corner bridle joint on the author's storm door has held together through a quarter century (and four kids). The pins keep the joint tight even if the glue should fail.

of adjusting the fence location to slice the cheek to the proper thickness after locating a stop block to arrest forward motion of the workpiece as soon as the blade enters the previously cut shoulder kerf. The stop block sits away from the fence enough to create an escape alley for the offcut pieces.

Corner Bridle Joint

A bridle joint is basically an "open" mortise-and-tenon joint. On a corner bridle joint, a two-shoulder tenon mates with a full-width mortise that's cut in from the end of the stock. It provides a very strong way to join frame corners, especially if the joint is pinned as well as glued. The only aesthetic objection to this joint is that the end of the

tenon shows at the edge of the workpiece. All the same, it's a very versatile utility joint.

Gary Rogowski, owner of the Northwest Woodworking Studio in Portland, Oregon, showed me a simple method for making a bridle joint. The setup guarantees a centered tenon that fits its mortise precisely. The trick to this method lies in using a shim that's the same thickness as the blade kerf. As shown on p. 181, one fence setting used in conjunction with the shim aligns all the cuts for both the tenon and mortise.

▶ See *"Bridle Joint"* on p. 181.

For efficient cutting, these identical brackets were stack-sawn all at once after taping the pieces together for the operation.

Stack sawing produced the individual maple, cherry, and mahogany parts for these cutting boards in one cutting operation.

Special Techniques

Bandsaws are capable of creating quite a variety of projects, all profiting from the saw's ability to cut curves and thick lumber. For example, multiple kitchen cutting boards and other panels made from curved pieces of contrasting wood can be created at the same time using the stack sawing technique. Bandsaw boxes are also very popular projects that make for great gifts.

[TIP] Although jigsaws and intarsia pictures can be cut on the bandsaw, the relatively wide kerf makes for ill-fitting pieces. Those projects are best done on a scroll saw.

Stack Sawing

Stack sawing is a great way to efficiently produce identical multiple pieces. The technique is a simple matter of temporarily affixing a stack of workpieces together for sawing, which cuts out all the pieces at once.

Stack sawing can also be employed to cut two or more layers of contrasting stock at the same time to produce interchangeable project parts in one cutting operation. The technique can be used to create interesting designs for cutting boards, drawer fronts, tabletops, or other panels. The process is easy. Simply secure the layers of various woods together with tape or hot-melt glue, draw your cut lines on the top layer or on an attached pattern, and saw out the parts. The pieces of contrasting wood can then be glued together in any combination you like.

▶ See *"Decorative Stack Sawing"* on p. 184.

Bandsaw Boxes

A bandsaw box can be made from a single block of wood using only a bandsaw for cutting out the drawers, framework, and outside shape. The block can be solid or laminated and can even be a split chunk of timber complete with natural edges. This clever technique creates all the parts for the box, including the body, the inner drawers, and the drawer faces. The wood grain runs continuously through all the parts, retaining the look of a solid chunk of wood.

The technique, shown on p. 185, provides a great opportunity to showcase highly figured

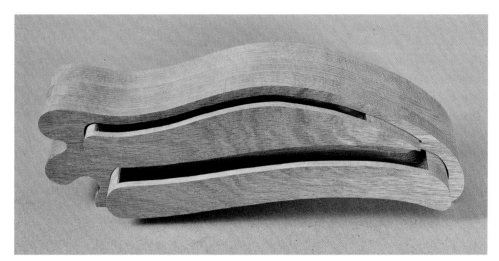

A bandsaw box showcases the ability of the bandsaw to produce very creative projects.

or spalted wood. It's also a good use for pieces with wormholes or other endearing characteristics that render them unusable for other projects. Firewood piles are great places to find wood with crotch grain or spalting. Just make sure the wood is sufficiently seasoned before you turn it into a box.

Jigs

A jig is a device that is used to help control the location or motion of a workpiece. The primary purpose of a jig is to control repeatability. Some jigs, such as a simple circle-cutting jig, are made for a single purpose and are often considered disposable after their initial intended use. Other jigs are designed to perform a specific task, but they incorporate enough adjustability that they will operate well with a wide range of stock sizes.

► See *"A Basic Circle-Cutting Jig"* on p. 155.

Featherboard Cutting Jig

A featherboard is a device for holding stock against a machine fence to ensure accuracy and improve safety. To provide adequate, consistent pressure on workpieces, feather-

A featherboard, with its long, thin fingers, provides a way to hold stock firmly against fences on tablesaws and other machines.

boards rely on accurately spaced fingers of consistent thickness. Laying out the fingers and sawing them freehand can lead to inaccuracy and tedium, so I made a jig to speed up the process.

► See *"Featherboard Cutting Jig"* on p. 187 and *"Making a Featherboard"* on p. 189.

This jig for making featherboards slides in the saw's miter gauge slots. The projecting fin registers every previous cut to ensure consistent spacing of a featherboard's kerfs.

These three identical brackets were quickly and accurately pattern-sawn by attaching the thin template to the workpiece and then guiding it along the end of the pattern jig arm.

The jig is a simple plywood panel that runs in the saw's miter gauge slot. It has a projecting fin to register every previous saw cut, which ensures evenly spaced fingers.

Pattern Sawing

Pattern sawing provides an easy way to create multiple identical parts by attaching a thin template to the workpiece blank and then guiding the edge of the template against a cantilevered jig arm that's clamped to the table.

The blade nestles in a notch in the end of the arm, which sits just above the workpiece blank. A plywood or hardboard template attached to the workpiece is guided along the end of the arm, sawing the edge of the stock flush to the edge of the template.

▶ See *"Pattern Sawing"* on p. 190.

The jig is easy to construct and the setup is simple. Just make sure to use a high-tpi blade that is sized to suit the tightest curve of the project. This type of sawing is usually followed directly by finish sanding to produce a smooth cut.

Log Sawing Sled

Most woodworkers have a natural fascination with making boards from logs. It's mesmerizing to watch a sawyer at the mill turn logs into lumber, revealing the beautiful variety of wood grain with every pass of the log carriage.

Bandsaws allow us to be sawyers in our own shops. The logs from a neighbor's dying apple tree are typically too small to be of interest to a professional sawyer, but they may be the perfect size for your bandsaw.

I've devised a slabbing sled that can handle logs up to 12 in. in diameter and 36 in. long, which are about as large as I can physically handle by myself. It consists of a base that rides in the table slot and a couple of end supports with adjustable anchor plates for attaching a log and presenting its edge to the blade.

The jig is quick to set up and use. A distinct advantage to this particular sled is that it will handle odd-shaped logs such as crotches and burls in addition to cylindrical pieces.

▶ See "Using a Log Sawing Sled" on p. 194.

This adjustable log-sawing jig does a great job of slabbing everything from cylindrical sections to odd-shaped crotches and burls.

▶ TIPS FOR SLABBING LOGS

Unless you intend to retain the bark on boards for a rustic look, it's a good idea to remove it before sawing a log into boards. Dirt and debris in the bark can quickly dull a good blade. It's also easier to see nails or other blade biters on the surface of a skinned log. Use compressed air to clean out checks and cracks, and trim the ends of the log to create a freshly sawn, square end. After sawing, stack the boards with consistently spaced stickers to minimize warping and aid proper seasoning.

Use a drawknife to remove blade-dulling bark before sawing a log. After sawing, sticker the boards to allow airflow between them and to protect the stack from direct sun and inclement weather.

A

B

Basic Cut-and-Tape Compound Sawing

To cut a workpiece with compound curves, begin by making full-scale patterns of the part's front and side profiles **(A)**. (In the case of this cabriole leg, both profiles are identical.) Transfer the patterns onto adjacent faces of the stock, taking care to orient them in the proper direction **(B)**. Saw the first profile **(C)**, and then tape the parts back together **(D)**. Continue the cut lines across the tape to prevent the possibility of wandering away from the lines **(E)**. Saw the second profile **(F)**, and remove the scrap to reveal your roughed-out workpiece, which is now ready for final shaping and sanding **(G)**.

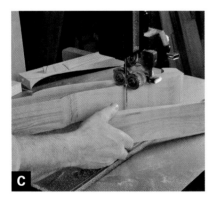

C

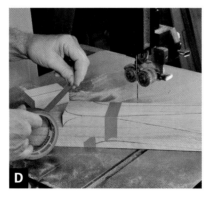

D

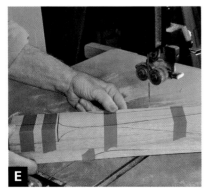

E

F

G

"Four-Square" Compound Sawing

With the "four-square" technique for compound sawing, each profile is sawed into two pieces, and then the pieces are switched in position and reassembled to create a different, final profile.

Begin by dressing your stock straight and square. This is important because the outside corners are ultimately joined together at the center of the piece. If the edges aren't square, the final, quartered lamination will have gaps.

Draw the profiles on two adjacent faces of the stock **(A)**. Keep in mind that a single cut line must be drawn on each face, resulting in parallel edges **(B)** after the parts are cut out. With this technique, you cannot taper parts nor lay out two different shapes on a face of the stock. Draw marks on the end of the stock at all four corners to help you orient the pieces after cutting the curves **(C)**.

Saw the cut line on one of the stock faces **(D)**. Tape the two pieces back together in their original configuration **(E)**, and saw the cut line on the adjacent face **(F)**. Reassemble the four pieces with the marked corners at the center **(G)**. If your outside corners were square, the resulting laminations should be nearly imperceptible **(H)**, resulting in a unique curved assembly **(I)**.

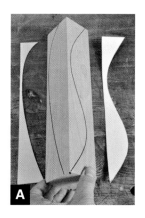
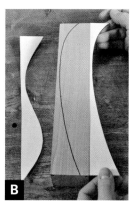
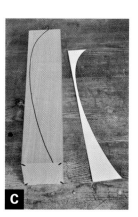

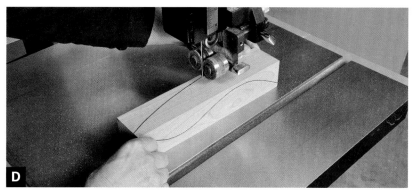

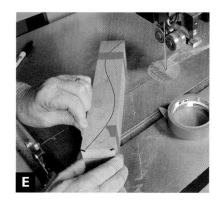
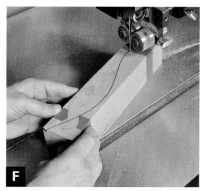

A

B

C

Curved Cock Beading

Curved cock beading can be created easily by sawing the bead from the panel to which it will be reattached, reducing the panel thickness, and then gluing the full-thickness bead back on.

Start by choosing panel stock that is the thickness of the desired cock bead. For this example, I wanted a 1/2-in.-thick panel with a 3/16-in. overhang, meaning I needed to start with 11/16-in.-thick stock. Finish-sand the face of the stock before starting, as the cock beading will impede easy sanding after assembly. Identify the back of the piece with a mark of some sort.

Mark the outside of the finished shape, including the cock beading **(A)**. Keep in mind that you will lose the thickness of the blade kerf during the process, so if the finished piece needs to be a specific size, be sure to account for the lost kerf width.

Carefully saw to the cut line **(B)**, and then sand, scrape, or plane the saw marks off the freshly sawed edge. Set up a single-point fence, locating the nose of the fence away from the blade at a distance equal to the thickness of the cock bead **(C)**. Then saw the cock bead from the panel stock **(D)**.

See *"Setting Up a Single-Point Fence"* on p. 122.

To round the edge of this 1/8-in.-wide cock bead, I used a table router outfitted with a bearing-guided 1/8-in.-radius router bit. A table-mounted guide pin helps steady the workpiece for starting the cut, while a push pad holds the work against the router bit and bearing. Two passes—one on each side—will result in a bullnose profile **(E)**. Afterward, sand away any burn marks or other irregularities on the exposed sections of the cock bead. However, don't sand the edge that mates with the panel edge.

Rip the panel to the desired thickness (in this case, ½ in.) **(F)**. When sawing, orient the pre-sanded front of the panel against the fence. Then glue the cock bead to the panel. By flushing up the back side of the two pieces, the overhang of the cock bead should be uniform along its length. Masking tape provides sufficient clamping pressure and readily conforms to irregular shapes **(G)**. After the glue is thoroughly dry, sand or plane the back side of the piece.

D

E

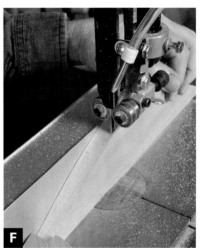

F

G

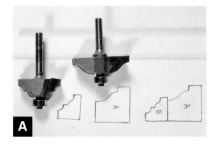

A

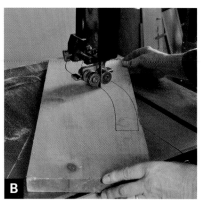

B

C

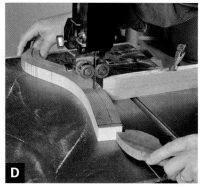

D

E

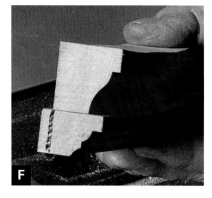

F

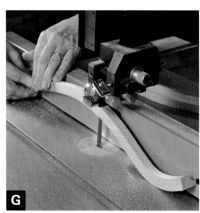

G

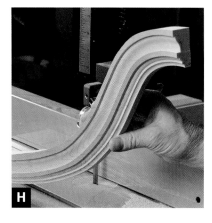

H

Curved Built-Up Moldings

Curved, built-up moldings are created in much the same manner as the curved cock beading discussed on pp. 174–175. The difference is that once the pieces are cut apart, the edges of the curved parts are molded on the router and the parts are trimmed to different widths to create setbacks or overhangs between pieces for enhanced reveals and shadow lines. Once molded, they are reassembled to produce the finished molding.

Start by drawing the end profile of the desired molding and determining where the section lines will be **(A)**. The section lines should land wherever there is a setback or overhang that can't be created with a standard router bit. Next, draw the molding's face profile, making sure the outside lines are parallel throughout the length of the molding. Tapered parts will compromise the molding profile, resulting in less than acceptable results. When laying out the cut lines, allow for a bit of excess to account for the loss of material to the saw kerf and sanding.

Each different profile cutter will determine a cut line for the molding blank. Keep in mind that the adjoining profiled parts can be adjusted fore and aft in profile to create interesting reveals.

Saw the blank **(B)**, and then smooth the inner edge, which is the surface that will guide the profile cutter **(C)**. Draw the section cut line, gauging it from the inside edge. Carefully saw freehand to the cut line, or use a single-point fence for better accuracy **(D)**. Mold the edges using a router or shaper **(E)**. Check the overlap for the correct reveal **(F)** and rip the section to its finished width **(G)**.

Glue the two pieces back together, keeping the rear faces flush to each other **(H)**. Take care not to apply too much glue, as squeeze-out can create finishing problems. Use a wet cloth to completely remove any excess.

Sawing Round Tenons

All you need to saw a round tenon on the end of a spindle is a rip fence, a shopmade V-cradle, and a piece of scrap to serve as a stop block **(A)**. Clamp the cradle to the fence about ⅛ in. in front of the blade's teeth. Position the stop block so that it sits behind the teeth at a distance equal to the length of the desired tenon, and then clamp it to the fence **(B)**.

Adjust the fence so that the bottom of the "V" in the cradle sits away from the teeth at a distance of exactly half the diameter of the desired tenon. Rather than measuring from the body of the blade, measure over from the side of a tooth that is set toward the cradle center **(C)**. When taking this measurement, take care to avoid side pressure on the blade, which can result in an inaccurate cut.

Use a piece of sacrificial stock to test the setup. Push the stock into the blade until it contacts the stop block. Retract the piece, rotate it slightly counterclockwise, and make the next cut alongside the first **(D)**. Continue cutting and rotating in this fashion **(E)** until you have completely sawed the tenon by rotating it a full 360°.

To clean up the shoulder, fully rotate the stock counterclockwise while holding it firmly in the cradle with its end butted against the stop block **(F)**. Check the fit of this test piece in a properly sized hole, and readjust the setup if necessary by sliding the fence sideways until the correct diameter is achieved.

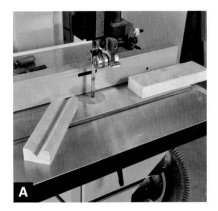

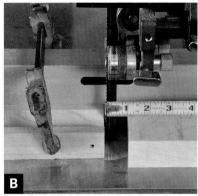

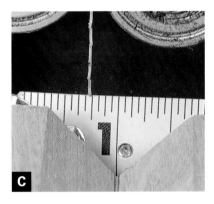

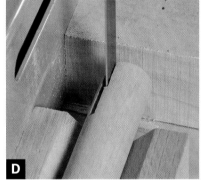

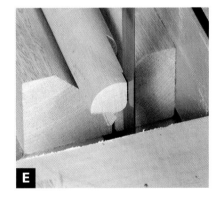

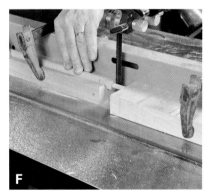

TENON SHOULDER JIG

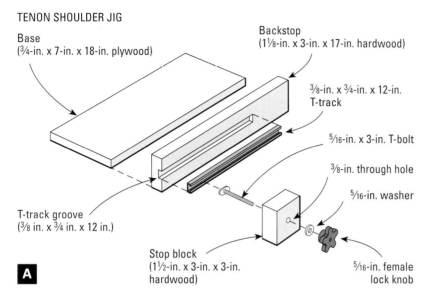

Base
(¾-in. x 7-in. x 18-in. plywood)

Backstop
(1⅛-in. x 3-in. x 17-in. hardwood)

⅜-in. x ¾-in. x 12-in.
T-track

⁵⁄₁₆-in. x 3-in. T-bolt

⅜-in. through hole

⁵⁄₁₆-in. washer

T-track groove
(⅜ in. x ¾ in. x 12 in.)

Stop block
(1½-in. x 3-in. x 3-in.
hardwood)

⁵⁄₁₆-in. female
lock knob

A

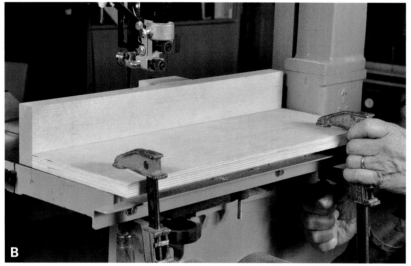

B

C

Tenon Shoulder Jig

This simple jig will create dead-on accurate tenon shoulders with crisp, clean cut lines. The blade is housed in a kerf in the backstop, allowing you to expose only the amount needed to cut to the exact shoulder depth. The adjustable stop, which locks onto a section of T-track, locates the workpiece for the desired tenon length.

Build the jig as shown in the drawing **(A)**, suiting the length of the backstop to the width of your bandsaw table for easy table attachment and to accommodate long tenons **(B)**. Then lay out and saw the blade housing kerf halfway through the backstop **(C)**.

To set up the jig, first use the miter gauge to square it to the blade and table **(D)**, and set your table clamps loosely in place. Next, adjust the backstop fore or aft to expose only the amount of blade needed to cut to the desired shoulder depth **(E)**. Then set the stop block for the desired tenon length **(F)**.

To make the cuts, use the miter gauge to push the workpiece tight to the backstop to saw the long shoulders **(G)** and the short ones **(H)**. Feed the work fairly briskly, particularly at the start. Hesitation may cause the blade to "hunt" a bit as it enters the wood, creating a fuzzy cut line. After each cut, carefully retract the stock in a straight line while holding it firmly against the miter gauge. This will prevent it from binding against the stop block and possibly ruining the cut or pulling the blade off track. Also, orient the stop block so the abutting edge is face grain instead of end grain, and wax the edge of the block. If you've done your work carefully, the operation will yield crisp shoulders cut to accurate depth **(I)**.

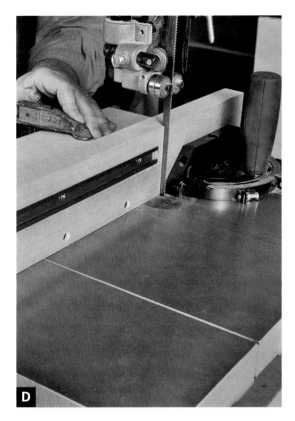

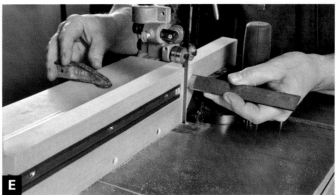

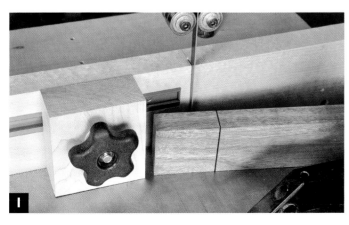

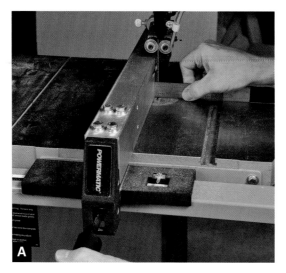

Sawing Tenon Cheeks

After sawing a tenon's shoulders as described on pp. 178–179, you're ready to cut the cheeks. First adjust the saw fence. Make sure it's square to the tabletop, and then position it for the cut, measuring from the fence to the opposite side of the blade **(A)**.

Clamp a stop block to the saw table to stop the workpiece travel as soon as the blade enters the shoulder kerf **(B)**. Locate the stop block away from the fence a distance equal to half the thickness of the workpiece (in this case, ⅜ in.). This creates an "escape alley" for the offcuts **(C)**. The stop material should be wide enough to allow the use of two clamps to keep the block from shifting upon contact with the workpiece.

Using scrap to check your setup, make a test cut, feeding the stock at a moderate rate. As you saw each shoulder, the previous offcut will be safely pushed into the escape alley **(D)**. The completed tenon should be neatly sawed, with smooth cheeks and crisp shoulders **(E)**.

Bridle Joint

Here is a quick, easy, and accurate way to make corner bridle joints on the bandsaw. The key to this method is using a thin shim to offset the workpiece by the width of a saw kerf when the tenon cheeks are being cut. The shim has to be exactly the thickness of the saw kerf. The easiest way to size it is to rip a kerf in a scrap, and then cut a shim that is a slight friction fit into the kerf **(A)**.

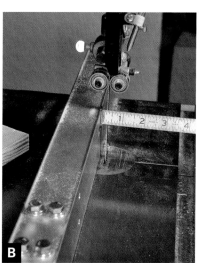

Here's how it works, using the example of dividing ¾-in.-thick stock into thirds for the joint segments. First, prepare to cut the mortise by setting the fence ¼ in. away from the blade **(B)**. Clamp a stop block to the table, butting it against the fence. The block should sit back of the teeth tips at a distance equal to the width of the stock **(C)**.

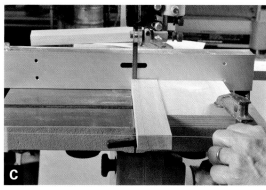

Saw the first mortise cheek, holding the stock tightly to the fence. Then flip the piece over to cut the opposite cheek **(D)**. Next, saw the tenon cheeks in the same fashion, except this time with the shim inserted between the fence and stock. As before, make the first cut **(E)**, and then flip the piece to make the second.

(continued on p. 182)

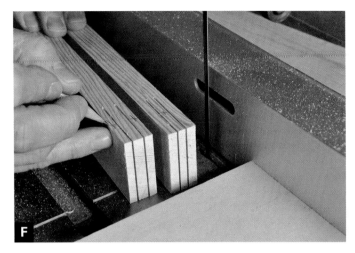

Before excavating the mortise waste and sawing the tenon shoulders, mark the waste to avoid cutting away the wrong sections **(F)**. Remove the mortise waste by taking a series of incremental straight slices, adjusting the fence for each subsequent cut. Make sure the stock completely abuts the stop block at the end of each cut **(G)**.

The last step is to saw the tenon shoulders. The most accurate and efficient approach is to use the tenon shoulder jig, as shown on p. 178. Alternatively, you can feed the stock with a miter gauge, using the fence as a stop to locate the shoulder cut **(H)**. When using this method, take care not to cut into the tenon itself. If you've done your work carefully, you should get a tight, accurate bridle joint every time **(I)**.

Basic Stack Sawing

Stack sawing can be used to reproduce multiple identical parts at the same time by temporarily attaching the part blanks in stacked fashion and then sawing them all at once.

Start by either drawing the design on one of the pieces or affixing a pattern to it **(A)**. Then tape the blanks together, judiciously locating the tape to keep the layers from shifting **(B)**. Saw out the profile, adding new tape as necessary to keep the blanks aligned as sections are cut away **(C)**. Take care to feed the cut line straight on to the blade to eliminate side pressure that can create an angled cut and mismatched parts.

After cutting out the complete shape, the brackets can be separated **(D)**. Alternatively, you can leave them taped together for stack sanding, relocating the tape as necessary to keep the blanks aligned as the sanding progresses.

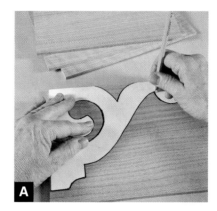

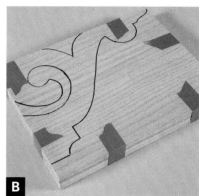

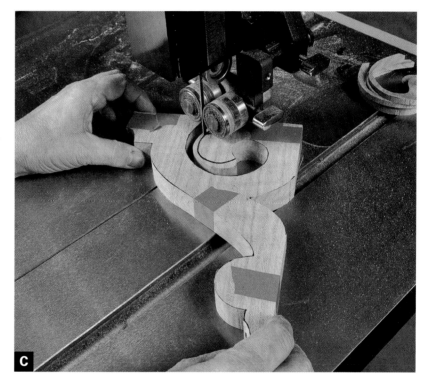

Decorative Stack Sawing

Decorative stack sawing is a great way to produce kitchen breadboards or other panels of curved contrasting woods. Boards of contrasting woods are stacked together for cutting, yielding identically shaped pieces that can then be reassembled in a combination of your choice. In this example, I'm using boards of maple, walnut, and mahogany **(A)** to make three cutting boards, which will each include all three woods.

If the finished panels need to be a specific size, make sure to allow for extra width and length to account for stock lost to saw kerfs and slight workpiece offsets. When laying out your cut lines, use long, sweeping arcs **(B)**, which will allow the best mating of the individual parts. Avoid S-curves, which will result in gaps between the parts due to the material lost by the saw kerf **(C)**.

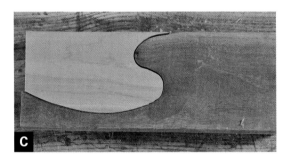

Tape the blanks together in such a way that the parts will remain attached after the cut. There's no need to fuss with the alignment of the board edges, as the panels will be trimmed to final size after assembly. Just make sure the parts won't shift during cutting. Saw to your cut lines **(D)**, feeding the stock steadily and smoothly to avoid glitches.

> **[TIP] A sacrificial backer/bottom layer will minimize tearout of the bottom piece. It will also provide additional support for thin or fragile pieces.**

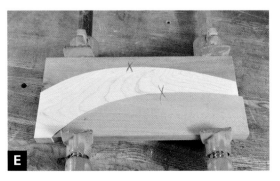

After sawing all the cut lines, remove the tape and rearrange the parts to create three panels of your chosen combination of woods. Align the parts for a good edge fit, and draw reference marks that straddle the joint line, which can be obscured by glue during clamp-up. Apply glue and clamp up the panels, keeping the marks aligned **(E)**.

Bandsaw Boxes

When making a bandsaw box, it's important to use a blade that's sized to suit the smallest radius curve of the box interior. Backing out of a cut or making relief cuts inside the box is usually not an option. It helps to use the drawing on p. 63 to select the appropriate blade size **(A)**. I use

> ► See *"Maximum Blade Widths for Curve Cuts"* on p. 63.

a ¼-in. 6-tpi blade almost exclusively for these projects. It's wide enough to cut reasonably straight, but narrow enough to cut fairly tight curves.

Start by slicing ¼ in. off the back of the squared box blank **(B)**. Set the piece aside because you'll reattach it later, but draw reference marks on it to identify its orientation in relation to the box body. Glue your pattern to the front of the block and cut out the drawer shapes. When entering the box body, saw parallel to the grain for easy glue-up and an invisible seam when reattaching the parts later **(C)**.

Label the top side of each drawer section to avoid confusion **(D)**. Cut the front and back off each drawer, typically slicing off ¼ in. or less **(E)**. Mark the desired drawer wall thickness on the section **(F)** before sawing out the drawer cavity. Relief cuts can be made to ease sawing the tight curves **(G)**.

(continued on p. 186)

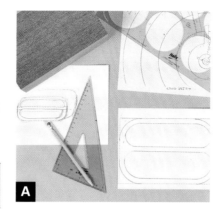

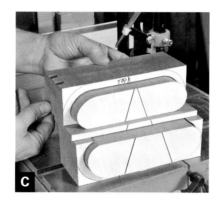

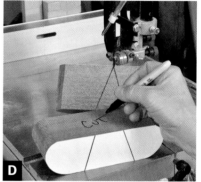

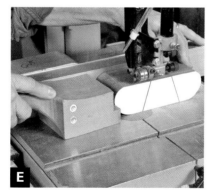

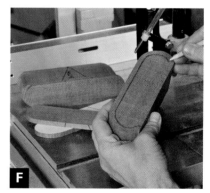

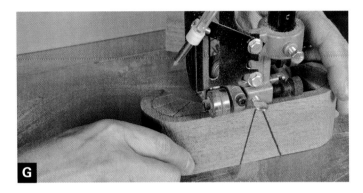

Glue the fronts and backs to the drawer bodies. Use clamp pads to help spread the pressure evenly and to prevent marring the drawer fronts **(H)**. I use liquid hide glue for bandsaw boxes. That way, if there is a slight misalignment while gluing up the many pieces, I can simply heat the parts to remove or realign them.

Reassemble the box body, again using clamping pads **(I)**. Cut the outside profile, and then trim the body to create a flush face with the finished drawers **(J)**. The box is now ready for final shaping and sanding **(K)**.

Featherboard Cutting Jig

This jig makes quick, accurate work of sawing evenly spaced fingers on a featherboard. It's just a plywood panel with a projecting fin to locate each previous cut for creating fingers of consistent spacing.

To build the jig, begin by cutting a ³⁄₄-in.-thick plywood panel to about 12 in. wide x 18 in. long. Place the center point of one end of the plywood against the blade, and mark the location of the table slot on the edge of the board **(A)**. Then mark out a hardwood runner for the jig and screw it to the bottom of the panel **(B)**.

With the panel riding in the table slot, saw about 4 in. into its leading edge **(C)**. This is the slot the blade rides in during operation. The next step is to cut the slot that accepts the locating fin. But first you'll need to decide how thick you want the fingers to be. I find that ¹⁄₈-in.-wide fingers about 2 in. long in ³⁄₄-in.-thick stock provide good support for general-purpose use. For less pressure, or when using thick stock, make the fingers longer and thinner. Conversely, for a stout featherboard, make fingers about ³⁄₁₆ in. wide and about 1¹⁄₂ in. long.

Flip the jig upside down and mark a line parallel to the saw kerf on the side facing away from the jig runner. Space the two apart by the desired width of your fingers **(D)**. Saw 4 in. into this line, using the bandsaw fence to ensure parallelism **(E)**.

(continued on p. 188)

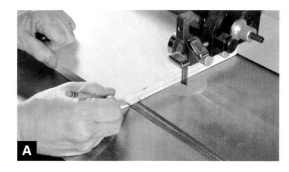

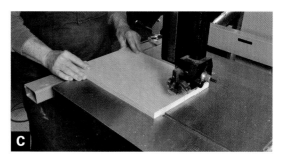

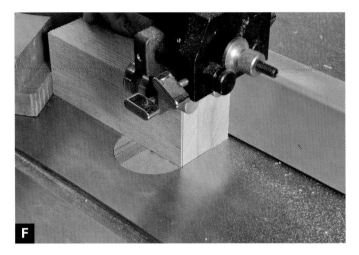

F

G

H

Rip the fin from the edge of a 1¼-in.-thick hard-wood block **(F)**, sizing it to fit snugly in the saw kerf without slop or binding. Then glue the fin into its slot, temporarily wedging unglued fin material into the adjacent blade slot **(G)**.

[TIP] **Using hide glue sparingly to attach the fin allows for easy replacement should it break.**

Finally, draw a series of parallel lines from the fin out to the edge of the board. Space them ¼ in. or so apart to serve as reference lines for parallel sawing **(H)**.

Making a Featherboard

It's easy to make a featherboard using the jig in the previous photo essay. First cut the featherboard blank to size, then draw a 30° angle on it to designate the finger baseline **(A)**. Use the jig to saw the featherboard fingers, hooking each previously cut kerf onto the fin to register the width of each subsequently cut finger.

To register the length of each cut, you can saw to the angled baseline, and then stop. However, with a few minutes of extra preparation, you can fine-tune the setup so that the fin stops each subsequent cut a bit farther back, automatically creating the angled baseline of cuts. It's a faster, more accurate approach. Here's how it works:

After drawing the angled baseline, mark out a few fingers that intersect the baseline. Then measure the distance between two adjacent intersections **(B)**. Using this measurement, mark a line back from the leading edge of the fin, and align the blade teeth to the mark **(C)**. Clamp the jig to the table at this location.

Cut the first finger by sliding the stock alongside the fin, stopping the cut at the baseline **(D)**. For all subsequent cuts, feed the stock forward with the fin riding inside the previous kerf as far as it will go **(E)**. After cutting all the fingers, trim the end of the featherboard at the same 30° angle as the baseline **(F)**.

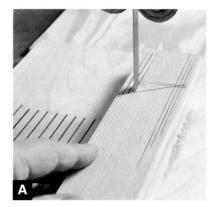

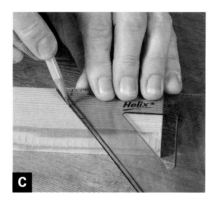

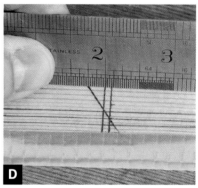

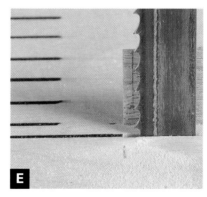

PATTERN SAWING JIG

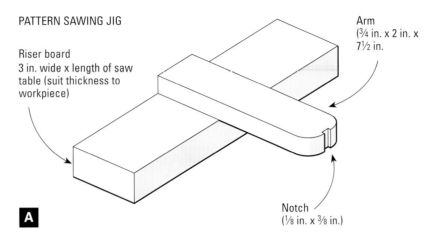

Riser board
3 in. wide x length of saw
table (suit thickness to
workpiece)

Arm
(¾ in. x 2 in. x
7½ in.)

Notch
(⅛ in. x ⅜ in.)

A

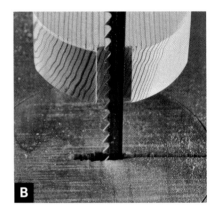

B

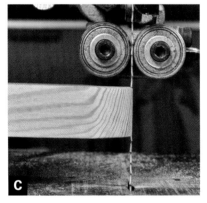

C

D

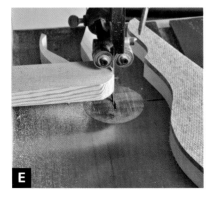

E

Pattern Sawing

To perform pattern sawing, you'll need to cobble together a simple jig with a cantilevered arm that provides a bearing surface for the edge of a template. A notch in the end of the arm houses the blade in use so that the workpiece edge is cut flush to the template edge. (If tight curves are involved, reduce the width of the arm at its end.) Outfit your saw with a ¼-in. or narrower blade.

Make the jig as shown in the drawing **(A)**. The length of the riser board should span the front-to-back depth of your saw table for easy clamping. Make it just a bit thicker than the stock you'll be sawing. Shape the arm, rounding its nose and cutting in the ⅛-in.-deep x ⅜-in.-wide blade notch at the tip. Screw the arm to the riser to allow easy reattachment to a different spacer when sawing thicker or thinner stock.

Clamp the pattern sawing jig to your saw table with the blade nestled in the arm notch **(B)**. Fine-tune the jig's position so that the end of the arm sits flush with the outer edge of the blade **(C)**.

Mount your template to the workpiece, and rough-cut the excess stock away to avoid interference with the riser board. Then start the trimming cut, keeping the template tight to the end of the arm **(D)**. The edges on the resulting workpiece should be flush to the edges of the template **(E)**.

Log Sawing Sled

This log sawing sled consists of a plywood base that slides fore and aft, guided by the saw table slot. Two upright end supports attach to the base. The one at the front adjusts fore and aft on T-tracks, while the one at the rear is fixed in place. Attached to each support is a plywood anchor plate that gets screwed to the ends of the log being cut. The anchor plates adjust laterally so that you can shift a log inward toward the blade to slice each new board in turn.

Begin by making the base as shown in the drawing **(A)**. Use Baltic birch or other good-quality hardwood plywood. After cutting the piece to size, saw the two 24-in.-long dadoes for the T-tracks and the ¼-in.-deep dado across the rear end, which will accept the bottom edge of the rear end support.

Square up the ends of the T-track dadoes, and insert the track, making sure it sits dead flush with the surface of the plywood **(B)**. Drill and countersink the track to accept at least four ½-in.-long screws, and then fasten the tracks in their dadoes. If the screw tips protrude a bit through the underside of the base, file them flush. (I use brass screws, which won't scar my saw table.)

Make a 48-in.-long hardwood runner that fits snugly in your table slot without side-to-side play. Screw the runner to the bottom of the base, positioned so that the edge of the base will sit about ⅛ in. from the blade with the runner in the table slot. My table has inverted T-slots, so I attach to the runner's fender washers that nestle in the slots to prevent the base from tilting off the table. To keep the runner straight during attachment, I clamp a straightedge alongside **(C)**. I also screw a 1x2 hardwood stiffener to the underside of the panel at the table edge to add strength and stability **(D)**.

(continued on p. 192)

LOG SAWING JIG

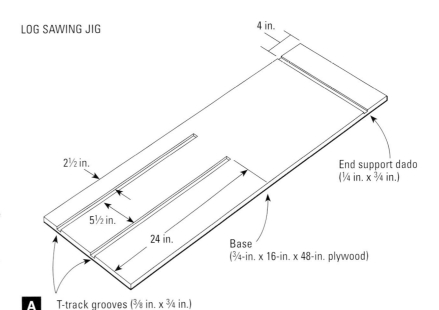

4 in.

2½ in.

5½ in.

24 in.

End support dado (¼ in. x ¾ in.)

Base (¾-in. x 16-in. x 48-in. plywood)

A   T-track grooves (⅜ in. x ¾ in.)

B

C

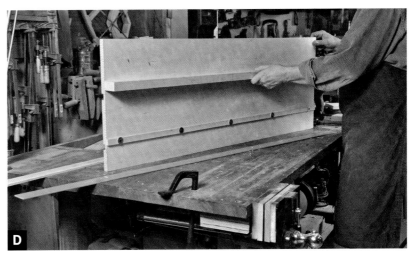

D

LOG SAWING JIG END SUPPORTS

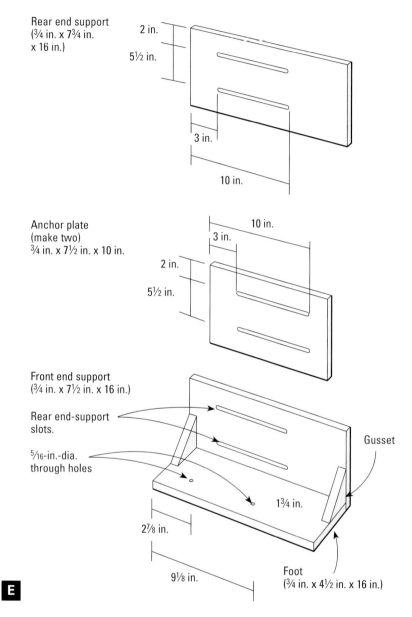

Rear end support
(³⁄₄ in. x 7³⁄₄ in.
x 16 in.)

2 in.

5½ in.

3 in.

10 in.

Anchor plate
(make two)
³⁄₄ in. x 7½ in. x 10 in.

10 in.

3 in.

2 in.

5½ in.

Front end support
(³⁄₄ in. x 7½ in. x 16 in.)

Rear end-support
slots.

⁵⁄₁₆-in.-dia.
through holes

Gusset

1³⁄₄ in.

2⅞ in.

9⅛ in.

Foot
(³⁄₄ in. x 4½ in. x 16 in.)

E

Make the end supports and anchor plates next, as shown in the drawing. All four pieces include two ³⁄₈-in.-wide x 7-in.-long horizontal slots to allow lateral movement of the anchor plates. You can either rout the slots or gang-drill their ends at the drill press **(F)**, and then connect the holes using a jigsaw **(G)**.

Screw the rear end support into its dado. To strengthen it and keep it square to the base, attach a couple of triangular gussets **(H)**, screwing in from the bottom of the base and the inner face of the end support.

[TIP] Assembling the jig without glue makes it easier to replace damaged parts in the future.

The front end support includes a foot for attachment to the base T-tracks using lock knobs. Saw the foot to shape, drill its lock knob holes, and then screw it to the end-support panel. As with the rear end support, add gussets for strength. Apply self-adhesive measuring tape to the top edge of each support **(I)**. For easy readability, use a standard "right-hand" tape for the rear support, with the numbers increasing as they approach the blade. Use a "left-hand" tape for the front support, with the numbers increasing in similar fashion. (See photo G on p. 195.) The increments allow easy indexing of the anchor plates as they are moved toward the blade for each successive cut.

Mount the front end support to its T-track using ⁵⁄₁₆-in. T-bolts with washers and lock knobs. Then attach the anchor plates to their end supports with ⁵⁄₁₆-in. machine bolts, washers, and lock knobs **(J)**.

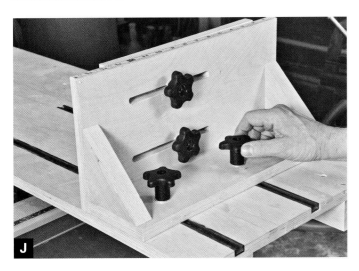

Using a Log Sawing Sled

Using the sled is a simple matter of screwing the anchor plates to the ends of the log, adjusting the log overhang for the desired thickness of slab, securing the lock knobs, and making the cut.

To ensure good anchor plate contact, you may first have to shim any angled ends on a log. To do this, gauge the angle using a T-bevel, with the log sitting in its intended cutting orientation **(A)**. Then saw a thick, wedge-shaped shim to that angle, and screw it to the end of the log **(B)**.

Screw the anchor plates to the log, working on a bench. With the lock knobs loosened, slide the plates to the left so they extend out from their end supports. Drill and countersink at least three holes for #8 screws, insetting the row of holes about ½ in. in from the edge of each anchor plate.

Now you're ready to attach the log. Working first from the rear end, screw through the anchor plate into the end of the log (or the shim) using 2½-in.-long #8 screws **(C)**. Make sure the screws enter the log at its vertical center. Next, do the same at the front end. When you're done, position the log so it's not overhanging the "blade edge" of the jig, and secure the lock knobs **(D)**. Outfit your saw with an appropriate blade. I typically use a ¾-in. 3-tpi hook-tooth blade for green wood and a ½-in. 6-tpi hook-tooth for dry wood. Set the guides for resawing, with the primary emphasis on correctly adjusted thrust bearings.

▶ See *"Setting the Blade Guides"* on p. 43.

Slide the jig onto the bandsaw table and adjust the log position so it overhangs the edge of the jig by the amount of the desired board width **(E)**, **(F)**. For reference, sight down the log toward the blade, and then use the tape measures on the end supports to ensure proper alignment **(G)**. Secure the lock knobs, start the saw, and feed the jig past the blade at an appropriate feed rate. After each pass, move the log over the desired distance by referencing the tape measures on the end supports to ensure consistency of thickness. Continue to saw boards until you're just shy of the middle of the log **(H)**.

At this point, remove the log, reverse it, and reattach it to the anchor plates with the sawed face toward the inside of the jig. Use a square to set the sawed face perpendicular to the jig base **(I)**. Set up for your first cut using the tape measures on the end supports. For example, in this case I wanted ³⁄₄-in.-thick slabs, so I set the edge of the anchor plate 3¼ in. in from the edge of the end supports **(J)**. This setting will yield four ³⁄₄-in.-thick pieces (totaling 3 in.), with the remaining ¼ in. factored in for the width of the saw kerfs.

After making the initial cut to this setting, move through the sawing process in the same manner you did when sawing the opposite side of the log. You should end up with a center board of relatively consistent thickness **(K)**.

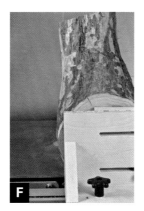

Glossary

Barrel cut (See *bellied cut.*)

Beam strength Resistance to deformation along the width of a bandsaw blade.

Bellied cut A cut that curves between the top and bottom of a board, forming a belly or bow. It's usually as a result of an under-tensioned blade or one with a pitch too fine for the wood thickness being cut. Also called a *bowed* or *barrel* cut.

Bimetal blade A blade that consists of a strip of high-speed steel welded to the edge of a spring steel body. When the teeth are cut, the high-speed steel remains as the points of the teeth.

Blade back The back edge of the blade body.

Blade body The steel ribbon that constitutes the bandsaw blade. The teeth are either attached or cut into the blade body.

Blade drift The propensity for a blade to cut out-of-parallel with a squarely set rip fence. Often caused by a dull or poorly supported blade.

Blade guides A set of blocks, wheels, or rollers that control side-to-side and fore-and-aft blade movement. One set typically sits above the table, and one sits below.

Blade tension Pressure applied outward on a blade by the upper wheel assembly, reinforcing the blade's beam strength and aiding in proper blade tracking of the wheels.

Blade thickness The thickness of the blade body.

Blade width The width of the blade body from tooth point to back edge.

Block guides Blade guides in the form of small blocks made from various materials, including ceramic, phenolic resin, plastic, steel, or wood.

Blowout A malfunction where the blade exits the side of the board, particularly during resawing.

Bowed cut (See *bellied cut.*)

Carbide blade A spring steel blade body with carbide teeth attached to it for a long-lasting cutting edge.

Carbon steel Iron with carbon added to form a high-strength material.

Ceramic Low-friction, long-wearing material used for blade guides.

Crosscut A cut made 90° to the direction of the grain.

Crown A slight radius on a bandsaw tire, designed to help track the blade.

Drift The tendency of a blade to cut out-of-parallel to a squarely set rip fence.

ETS Every tooth set. Also referred to as *alternate set.*

European-style guides Blade guides that consist of side wheels with their faces set parallel to the blade, as well as a rear wheel set perpendicular to the blade. The wheels are mounted on axles that run in bushings.

Feed rate The rate that material is pushed past the blade, measured in feet per minute (fpm).

Flex back A non-hardened spring steel blade body. A flex back blade can have hardened teeth to create a *hard-edge* blade.

Flutter Rhythmic vibrations of the blade during the cutting procedure.

Guide bearings Guides that rotate with the blade while supporting and guiding it; used to provide side and/or thrust support.

Guide blocks Rectangular or round blocks of wood, plastic, metal, ceramic, or phenolic material that provide blade guidance and support. Also called *rub blocks.*

Guidepost The vertically adjustable post that carries the upper blade guides.

Gullet The space between blade teeth, designed to evacuate sawdust.

Gullet depth The distance from tooth point to the bottom of the gullet.

Hard back A blade with an induction-hardened rear edge for increased durability and beam strength.

Hard edge A blade with flame- or induction-hardened teeth for increased durability and abrasion resistance.

High-speed steel High-carbon steel with various compounds added to increase hardness, toughness, or heat resistance.

Hook-tooth A tooth having a positive rake angle.

Induction hardening A process by which the teeth and/or back of a blade are heated electrically and then quenched to create a harder wear surface, while leaving the blade body unaffected, for better flexibility and longer life.

Kerf The width of the cut made by a blade.

M2 high-speed steel The type of high-speed steel typically used to produce woodcutting bimetal blades.

Modified raker set A tooth pattern consisting of one unset tooth followed by two pairs of alternately set teeth in a repeating sequence.

Phenolic Synthetic thermosetting resin used for making self-lubricating blade guides.

Phenolic blade guides Self-lubricating blade guides that can operate in direct contact with the blade.

Pitch The number of teeth per inch (tpi) on a bandsaw blade.

Point The tip of the tooth, which does the actual cutting of the wood fibers.

Positive rake angle A tooth whose face is acutely angled in relation to the blade's axis; characteristic of a *hook*-tooth.

PSI Pounds per square inch; a measurement of pressure.

Rake angle The angle of the tooth face in relation to the blades' axis.

Raker set A tooth pattern consisting of one unset tooth followed by a pair of alternately set teeth in a repeating sequence.

Regular tooth A type of blade that typically has evenly spaced teeth with a zero rake angle.

Relief cut A cut extending from the waste to the cut line, used to free the waste in sections for better blade maneuverability, especially when cutting curves.

Resaw Cutting a thick board into thin sheets or panels by sawing across the width of the board.

Resaw height The vertical distance between the tabletop and the upper blade guides at their highest setting; the maximum thickness of stock the saw is capable of sawing. Also called *throat height*.

Rip cut A cut made along the length of the grain.

Rip fence A fence running front-to-back across the saw table used for guiding boards during rip cuts.

Rockwell hardness (Rc) A scale that rates the hardness of metal; higher numbers indicate greater hardness.

Roller guides Side and thrust guides that use ball bearings to control and direct the blade.

Rub blocks Guide blocks that help control a blade by providing direct contact against its sides.

Set (See *tooth set*.)

Side guides Blade guides located to either side of the blade, usually above and below the table, to help prevent lateral blade motion and twisting.

Skip tooth A tooth pattern with wide spacing between the teeth.

Spring steel Carbon steel that has been modified with an alloy.

Table The flat working surface surrounding the blade.

Table insert A removable plate that surrounds the blade where it threads through the table.

Teeth The points on a blade that do the cutting.

Tension (See *blade tension*.)

Tension gauge A device that reads the amount of tension placed on the blade by the saw's wheels.

Throat height (See *resaw height*.)

Throat width The horizontal distance between the blade and the upper wheel support column.

Thrust bearing Bearings located behind the blade to restrict its rearward movement.

Tire The rubber covering on the wheel that the blade rides on.

Tooth face The underside edge of the tooth, which "faces" the work.

Tooth set The lateral flare of a tooth, which creates a kerf that's wider than the blade body to prevent binding and aid sawdust extraction.

Tooth spacing The distance between the teeth on a blade, also called *pitch*.

TPI Teeth per inch.

Tracking Positioning the blade relative to the width of the tire.

Trunnions The table supports that allow tilting it to make beveled cuts.

Variable pitch Teeth spaced at various intervals rather than in a constant repetitive pattern.

Wandering The tendency of a blade to cut erratically in relation to the cut line.

Wheel The rotating device on which the saw blade rides.

Wheel house The body of the saw surrounding the wheels.

Zero rake angle A tooth whose face is at 90° to the blade's axis.

Metric Conversion Chart

INCHES	CENTIMETERS	MILLIMETERS	INCHES	CENTIMETERS	MILLIMETERS
1/8	0.3	3	13	33.0	330
1/4	0.6	6	14	35.6	356
3/8	1.0	10	15	38.1	381
1/2	1.3	13	16	40.6	406
5/8	1.6	16	17	43.2	432
3/4	1.9	19	18	45.7	457
7/8	2.2	22	19	48.3	483
1	2.5	25	20	50.8	508
1 1/4	3.2	32	21	53.3	533
1 1/2	3.8	38	22	55.9	559
1 3/4	4.4	44	23	58.4	584
2	5.1	51	24	61.0	610
2 1/2	6.4	64	25	63.5	635
3	7.6	76	26	66.0	660
3 1/2	8.9	89	27	68.6	686
4	10.2	102	28	71.1	711
4 1/2	11.4	114	29	73.7	737
5	12.7	127	30	76.2	762
6	15.2	152	31	78.7	787
7	17.8	178	32	81.3	813
8	20.3	203	33	83.8	838
9	22.9	229	34	86.4	864
10	25.4	254	35	88.9	889
11	27.9	279	36	91.4	914
12 1/2	30.5	305			

Resources

CARTER PRODUCTS
2871 Northridge Dr. NW
Grand Rapids, MI 49544
800-622-7837
www.carterproducts.com
Bandsaw guides, blades, and accessories

DELTA MACHINERY
4825 Hwy. 45 North
Jackson, TN 38305
800-223-7278
www.deltaportercable.com
Bandsaws

EAGLE TOOLS
3027 Treadwell St.
Los Angeles, CA 90065
323-999-2909
www.eagle-tools.com
Agazzani bandsaws, Inca bandsaw parts

FELDER-GROUP, USA
866-792-5288
www.felderusa.com
Bandsaws

FENNER DRIVES
311 West Stiegel St.
Manheim, PA 17545
800-243-3374
www.fennerdrives.com
Segmented V-belts

GENERAL INTERNATIONAL
888-949-1161
www.general.ca
Bandsaws

GRIZZLY INDUSTRIAL, INC.
8121 Valencia St.
Bellingham, WA 98229
800-523-4777
www.grizzly.com
Bandsaws, blades, guides, and accessories

HARTVILLE TOOLS
13163 Market Ave. North
Hartville, OH 44632
800-345-2396
www.hartvilletool.com
Drawing supplies, adjustable

curves, T-track and accessories; bandsaw blades, guides, and accessories

HIGHLAND WOODWORKING
1045 N. Highland Ave. NE
Atlanta, GA 30306
800-241-6748
www.highlandwoodworking.com
Bandsaws, blades, guides, and accessories

HITACHI POWER TOOLS
800-706-7337
www.hitachipowertools.com
Benchtop bandsaws

HTC PRODUCTS
6520 Bethuy
Fair Haven, MI 48023
800-624-2027
www.htcproductsinc.com
Mobile bases

ITURRA DESIGN
4636 Fulton Rd.
Jacksonville, FL 32225
904-642-2802
Bandsaw accessories

JET TOOLS
427 New Sanford Rd.
La Vergne, TN 37086
615-793-8900
www.jettools.com
Bandsaws

LAGUNA TOOLS
17101 Murphy Ave.
Irvine, CA 92614
800-234-1976
www.lagunatools.com
Bandsaws, blades, guides, and accessories

MAGCRAFT
National Imports LLC
1934 Old Gallows Rd.
Suite 350
Vienna, VA 22182
888-774-6005
www.magcraft.com
Rare-earth magnets

MINI-MAX USA
2475 Satellite Blvd.
Duluth, GA 30096
866-975-9663
www.minimaxusa.com
Bandsaws

OLSON SAW COMPANY
16 Stony Hill Rd.
Bethel, CT 06801
203-792-8622
www.olsonsaw.com
Bandsaw blades, guides, and accessories

POWERMATIC
800-274-6848
www.powermatic.com
Bandsaws

RIDGID TOOLS
800-474-3443
www.ridgid.com
Bandsaws, blades, and accessories

RIKON TOOLS
16 Progress Rd.
Billerica, MA 01821
877-884-5167
www.rikontools.com
Bandsaws and accessories

ROCKLER WOODWORKING AND HARDWARE
4365 Willow Dr.
Medina, MN 55340
800-279-4441
www.rockler.com
Bandsaws, blades, guides, and accessories

RYOBI TOOLS
800-525-2579
www.ryobitools.com
Benchtop bandsaws

SPACEAGE CERAMICS
P.O. Box 929
Loomis, CA 95650
916-652-6302
www. spaceageceramicguide
blocks.com
Ceramic guide blocks

STEEL CITY TOOLWORKS
3656 Enterprise Ave.
Hayward, CA 94545
877-724-8665
www.steelcitytoolworks.com
Bandsaws

SUFFOLK MACHINERY CORPORATION
12 Waverly Ave.
Patchogue, NY 11772
800-234-7297
www.suffolkmachinery.com
Bandsaw blades

SUPERCUT
14283 N. Thayer St.
Rathdrum, ID 83858
800-356-9918
www.supercutbandsaw.com
Bandsaw blades, guides, and accessories

WEARWELL
800-264-3030
www.wearwell.ccom
Anti-fatigue mats

WOODCRAFT SUPPLY
1177 Rosemar Rd.
Parkersburg, WV 26102
800-535-4482
www.woodcraft.com
Bandsaws, blades, guides, and accessories

WOODWORKER'S SUPPLY
5604 Alameda Pl. NE
Albuquerque, NM 87113
800-645-9292
www.woodworker.com
Bandsaws, blades, guides, and accessories

Index

A

Accessories, 20–24, 87–89. *See also specific accessories*
Aligning components. *See* Tuning bandsaws
Anatomy of bandsaws, 11–20. *See also specific components*
  diagrams, 11, 12, 13
  frame types, 11–14
Anti-fatigue mats, 23–24
Arcs. *See* Sawing curves
Assessing old saws, 27–30

B

Backing out of cuts, 92–94, 141
Beam compasses, 130–31, 153–54
Bellied cuts, troubleshooting, 46–47
Belts and pulleys, 36–37
Benchtop saws, 8–9
Benefits of bandsaws, 4–5
Bevels, ripping, 106
Blade drift, 21, 37, 99, 117–18
Blade guards, 72, 81, 91
Blade guides, 68–81. *See also* Thrust guides/bearings
  about: overview of, 15, 68
  aftermarket, 76–78, 81
  basic types of, 69
  blade guard and, 91
  block guides, 69–72, 76, 80
  ceramic, 72, 77
  edge-bearing rollers, 73
  European-style, 74–75, 79
  face-bearing rollers, 73
  hardwood, 70
  for narrow blades, 139–40
  phenolic-impregnated, 71, 77
  plastic, 70–71, 77
  roller guides, 69, 72–75, 76–77
  setting, 43–44, 45, 97, 138–39
  specialty rollers, 78
  squaring, 79–80
  steel, 69–70
Blade tracking problems/solutions, 46
Blade(s), 54–67
  about: overview of, 54
  aligning wheels for, 32–35
  beam strength, 39

blowout, 47
bowed, bellied, rippled cuts, 46–47
breaking and repairing, 67, 89
burning or binding, 48
changing, 39–44, 87
cleaning, 66
direction, 90
flex, preventing, 100
folding, 52
heat-treated, 56
materials (types of steel), 54–57, 62
removing/mounting, 40–42
safety tips. *See* Safety
selecting, 62–65, 90
sharpness, 90
sources, 64, 198–99
specifications worksheet, 65
stoning, 49
storing, 66–67
teeth per inch (tpi) or pitch, 58, 59, 64
tension. *See* Tension
terminology, 54, 55
thickness and width, 61, 62–64
tooth manufacture, 58
tooth set, 60–61
tooth shape/type, 58–60, 64
troubleshooting issues, 45–48
by type of work, 65, 90 (*see also specific type of cut*)
vibration issues, 34–35, 46
wandering, 47–48
width and cut radius, 62
Block guides, 23, 49, 69–72, 76, 80
Blowout, 47
Body and hand position, 91–93
Bowed cuts, troubleshooting, 46–47
Bowl blanks, 7, 39
Boxes, bandsaw, 168–69, 185–86
Bridle joints, 7, 167, 181–82
Built-up curved moldings, 164–65, 176
Buying bandsaws
  additional resources for, 27, 30, 198–99
  checklists for, 26, 28
  new, considerations, 24–27
  used, assessing, 27–30

C

Cabriole legs. *See* Compound curves
Card scrapers, 145–46
Carter Stabilizers, 78
Cast-iron frames, 12–13
Ceramic guides, 72, 77
Circles. *See* Sawing curves
Cleaning
  bandsaws, 48–49
  blades, 66
Cock beading, curved, 164, 174–75
Compass (circular) planes, 146–47
Compasses, 130–31, 153–54. *See also* Sawing curves
Compound curves, 162–63, 172–73
Computer-generated patterns, 133
Coplanarity, 34
Crosscut sled, 127
Crosscutting, 110–11
Cut-and-tape method, 163, 172
Cutting abilities, 5–7. *See also* Ripping; *Sawing references*
Cutting capacity, 25
Cylindrical stock
  cradle jig for, 128
  crosscutting, 64
  ripping, 107
  V-blocks for, 89

D

Decorative stack sawing, 184
Die-cast frames, 11–12
Dovetails, 7, 166
Drift. *See* Blade drift
Drive mechanism, 17–19
Dust collection
  options, 86–87
  port, 19, 27
Dust masks, 86

E

Ear protection, 85
Ellipses and ovals, 135, 136, 159–61. *See also* Sawing curves
Eye protection, 85

F

Featherboards, 88, 89, 169–70, 187–89
Feeding stock, 93–94. *See also specific types of cuts*
Fences. *See Rip fences*
Flexible curves, 134. *See also Sawing curves*
Folding blades, 52
Foot brake, 20
Footprint, 5–6
"Four-square" compound sawing, 163, 173
14-in. stand-mounted saws, 9–10, 11
Frame types, 11–14
French curves, 133–34

G

Glossary, 196–97
Guide blocks. *See Block guides*
Guidepost
    checking flex of, 29
    components, illustrated, 11, 12, 72
    guides on, 68 (*see also Blade guides*)
    tuning up, 38–39
Guides, 15, 23, 25. *See also Blade guides; Thrust guides/bearings*

H

Hand position, 92–93
Hi-lo fence, making, 119
History of bandsaws, 6
Horsepower, 25

I

Inspecting used saws, 29
Installing aftermarket, 81
Iturra Bandrollers, 78

J

Jigs, about, 169. *See also specific jigs*
Joinery, 7, 65, 166. *See also Tenon(s)*

L

Lighting, 85
Location of saw, 84
Log sawing sleds, 7, 170–71, 191–95

M

Maintenance, general, 48–49. *See also Tuning bandsaws*
Miter gauge
    about: overview of, 16
    crosscutting with, 111
    functions of, 88
Mobile bases, 22–23
Moldings, curved built-up, 164–65, 176. *See also Cock beading, curved*

N

Notches, 3-sided, 116

O

Ovals, 135, 136, 160–61. *See also Sawing curves*

P

Pattern sawing, 170, 190–91
Phase of motors, 18, 30
Phenolic-impregnated guides, 71, 77
Plastic guide blocks, 70–71, 77
Power and power demands, 5, 25
Profile gauges, 134–35
Push blocks, 109, 113–14
Push sticks, 87–88, 109, 112

Q

Quick-release tension levers, 19, 22

R

Resawing, 7
    blades, 61–62, 65, 109
    blowout issues, 47
    guidelines, 108–09
    ripping compared to, 96
    riser blocks helping, 9, 22
    saws for, 9–11
Resources, 198–99
Rip fences
    about: overview of, 16
    adjusting for drift, 118
    aftermarket, 21
    hi-lo fence, 119
    making your own, 21, 119–21
    orienting workpiece to, 102–03
    single-point, *See Rip fences*
    using, 98–99

Rip fences (single-point)
    about, 98
    making, 120–21
    ripping with, 107–08
    setting up, 122
Ripping, 96–108
    bevels, 106
    blade drift and, 21, 37, 99, 117–18
    blades for, 65, 96–97
    crosscut sled for, 127
    curved stock, 105
    cylindrical stock, 107
    feeding stock, 100–101
    freehand, 101–02, 115
    guides for, 97
    live-edge (waney) material, 106
    multiples, 103–04
    narrow pieces, 104–05
    resawing compared to, 96
    setting up for, 96–100
    with single-point fence, 107–08
    squaring table to blade, 99–100
    with straight fence, 102–06
    taper jigs for, 123–26
    tapers, 106–07
    thin stock, 105
    using fences, 98–99 (*see also Rip fences references*)
Rippled cuts, troubleshooting, 46
Riser blocks, 9, 22
Roller guides, 69, 72–75, 76–77
Round stock. *See Cylindrical stock*

S

Safety, 82–94
    accessories, 87–89
    basics, 83
    changing blades, 87
    checklist, 89–91
    dust collection and, 86–87
    feeding stock, 93–94
    gear, 85–86
    knowing saw/reading manual, 82–83
    lighting and, 85
    saw placement and, 84
    stance (body and hand position), 91–93
    workstation and, 84–85
Sanding and smoothing, 143–49
    card scrapers for, 145–46
    compass (circular) planes for, 146–47
    hand sanding, 143–44
    hand-tooling, 145
    power sanders for, 147–48, 149

shopmade sanding files for, 145
spokeshaves for, 146
template routing and, 148–49
Sawing
    backing out of cuts, 92–94
    bowl blanks, 7, 39
    feeding stock safely, 93–94 (*see also specific types of cuts*)
    planning cut sequence, 94
    shapes, 5–7
    slabs. *See* Slabbing logs
    stance (body and hand position) for, 91–93
    straight cuts. *See* Resawing; Ripping; Sawing straight
    test cuts, 30, 102
    troubleshooting problems with, 45–48
Sawing curves, 129–61
    about: overview of, 129–30
    arc layouts, 130–33, 150–53
    backing out of cuts, 141
    bandsaw boxes, 168–69, 185–86
    basic procedures, 140–43
    blades for, 65, 137–38
    built-up moldings, 164–65, 176
    circles, 130–33, 141–42, 155–57
    cock beading, 164, 174–75
    compasses for, 130–31, 153–54
    complex curves, 142
    compound curves, 162–63, 172–73
    computer-generated patterns for, 133
    curve templates, 157–58
    cut-and-tape method, 163, 172
    drawing splines/flexible curves, 134
    ellipses and ovals, 135, 136, 159–61
    feeding stock, 141
    "four-square" method, 163, 173
    French curves, 133–34
    guides for, 138–40
    guiding narrow blades for, 139–40
    laying out circles and arcs, 130–33
    profile gauges and, 134–35
    radius of arcs, 131
    scroll cuts, 5, 25, 65, 92, 93, 94, 143
    setup for, 135–40
    simple curves, 141
    smoothing after, 143–49
    variable curves, 133–35
Sawing straight, 95–128. *See also* Resawing; Ripping
    about: overview of, 95–96
    crosscutting, 110–11
    handling blade drift, 117–18
    3-sided notches, 116

Scroll cuts, 5, 25, 65, 92, 93, 94, 143
16-in. and larger saws, 10–11
Sizes of saws, 7–11
Slabbing logs, 7, 171, 191–95
Sleds
    crosscut, 111, 127
    log sawing, 7, 170–71, 191–95
    small parts, 88
Small parts sleds, 88
Splines, drawing, 134
Spokeshaves, 146
Stack sawing, 168, 183–84
Steel, types of blades, 54–57
Stoning blades, 49
Supporting work, 84

T

Tables, bandsaw
    aligning and maintaining, 37–38, 99–100, 110
    auxiliary, 20
    checking flatness of, 29
    structure and functions, 15–16, 25–27
    trunnions and, 25–27
    zero-clearance inserts for, 53, 88, 89
Tablesaws vs. bandsaws, 4, 7, 82, 85, 95, 103, 166
Taper jigs, 123–26
Tapers, ripping, 106–07
Teeth. *See* Blade(s)
Template routing, 148–49
Templates, for circles/curves, 132–33, 157–58
Tenon(s), 165–67, 177–82
    bridle joints, 7, 167, 181–82
    cheeks, 7, 166–67, 180, 181
    four-shoulder, 166–67, 178–79
    ripping freehand, 101–02
    round, 166, 177
    shoulder jig, 178–79
Tension
    quick-release lever, 19
    quick-release retrofit, 22
    releasing between uses, 20
    safety precaution, 90–91
Tension gauges, 43
Tension spring failure, 42
Test cuts, 30, 102
3-sided notches, 116
Three-wheeled saws, 8
Thrust guides/bearings, 44, 47, 56, 97
    adjusting, 38–39, 44, 47
    aftermarket, 76–78, 81
    ceramic, 72

cleaning and lubricating, 40
edge-bearing and face-bearing, 73, 75
European-style, 74
functions of, 15, 68
illustrated, 25, 45, 69, 72
for narrow blades, 139–40
ripping and, 97
Tires. *See also* Wheels
    about, 14–15
    cleaning, 41
    grooved or loose, 35
    inspecting, 29–30
    recrowning, 35, 50
    releasing tension on, 19–20
    replacing, 51
Troubleshooting, 45–48
Tuning bandsaws
    about: overview of, 32
    aligning wheels, 32–35
    changing blades, 39–44, 87
    drive belts and pulleys, 36–37
    guidepost, 38–39
    replacing/repairing tires, 35, 50, 51
    setting blade guides, 43–44, 45, 97
    table, 37–38
    testing after, 45
    tools and materials for, 31–32
    troubleshooting and, 45–48
    truing guide blocks, 49
Types of saws, 7–11

V

V-blocks, for round stock, 89
Vibration, troubleshooting, 46

W

Wandering blades, 47–48
Welded-steel frames, 13, 14
Wheel adjusters, 17
Wheel house, 12, 13, 14
Wheels. *See also* Tires
    about, 14–15
    aligning, 32–35
    inspecting, 29–30
Workstation, 84–85

Z

Zero-clearance inserts, 53, 88, 89